# THE

## NORTHERN MONKEY SURVIVAL GUIDE

# THE

**NORTHERN MONKEY SURVIVAL GUIDE**

How to Hang on to Your
**NORTHERN CRED** in a World
Filled with **SOUTHERN JESSIES**

## TIM COLLINS

Michael O'Mara Books Limited

First published in Great Britain in 2009 by
Michael O'Mara Books Limited
9 Lion Yard
Tremadoc Road
London SW4 7NQ

Copyright © Michael O'Mara Books Limited 2009

A CIP catalogue record for this book is available from the British Library.

Papers used by Michael O'Mara Books Limited are natural, recyclable
products made from wood grown in sustainable forests. The manufacturing
processes conform to the environmental regulations of the country of origin.

ISBN: 978-1-84317-344-1

1 2 3 4 5 6 7 8 9 10

www.mombooks.com

Cover design by Blacksheep Design

Illustrations by Andrew Pinder

Design and typesetting by Envy Design

Printed and bound in Great Britain by Clays Ltd, St Ives plc

# CONTENTS

For Collette

# INTRODUCTION

'Remember that you are an Englishman and have consequently won first prize in the lottery of life.'
CECIL RHODES

Cecil Rhodes might have believed that being English was like winning the lottery, but there are times when being from the North of England feels more like winning a tenner on the scratchcard of life and spending it all on Special Brew.

We get called 'Northern Monkeys', even though only a tiny minority of us walk like primates, and most of those find work as lead singers in Manchester indie bands. Southerners mock us with greetings of 'Ey up chuck' and 'Ee by gum', even though we never actually use these phrases in real life. They have the nerve to cast suspicious glances our way if something in the office goes missing, even though we don't want their crappy stuff. And they joke about us using outdoor toilets, even though the only time you're likely to see anyone relieving themselves outdoors is in central London on a Saturday night, because all the public toilets have been converted into trendy restaurants and bijou flats.

All of this would count as racism if the North was a separate country. But it's not, so we have to grit our teeth while southerners mock us with their braying laughter.

Well maybe the time has come for us to fight back. The North is home to the best food, the best drink, the best music, the best football, the best prices, the best nights out and, more importantly, the best people in the country. Being northern is nothing to be ashamed of. In fact, it's those devious southerners who should apologize, for centuries of robbing our best ideas.

So if you're northern and proud, I hope you find this guide a celebration of everything that makes the North so great, and everything that makes the South so shite. It's time to grab a pint with a proper head on it, stick a ferret down your trousers and settle back for a celebration of the half of England that's cooler in more ways than one.

## ACKNOWLEDGEMENTS

Thanks to Craig Ainsley, Sarah Quinn, Dan Hulse, Mike Hughes, Jim Derwent, Lindsay Davies, Kerry Chapple, Ana Sampson and everyone at Michael O'Mara, and to all those Northern Monkeys who shared their inspirational stories about oppression by southerners.

# THE ORIGIN OF THE NORTHERN MONKEY SPECIES

**To find out how the Northern Monkey came about, we need to look back to the early history of the region, which was pretty much one big Saturday night out, with massive fights following by lots of shagging: wave after wave of invaders came over from Europe to kick our arses before eventually settling down and breeding with the locals.**

## The prehistoric Northern Monkey

Modern humans originally settled in the area in the Palaeolithic age, when Britain was still connected to the European land mass. This meant that you could walk over from France, which had the advantage that you could avoid visiting Dover. Over the next few thousand years, peoples such as the Celts wandered over and settled in the North.

Around 5000 BC, the sea rose over the bit of land that connected us to Europe. This must have been especially annoying if you were planning to cross but didn't make it in time. Not only would you have to drastically rethink your settlement plans, but you'd be French. An island was now formed that would become home to the separate countries of Scotland, Wales, Northernmonkeyland and Southernjessieland.

## Simius Romanus

In AD 43, the Romans invaded Britain. Although they went as far as Scotland at one point, they eventually retreated to the far north of what is now England, with Emperor Hadrian ordering the building of his famous wall to mark the northern frontier of the Roman Empire. The Romans brought many conveniences that southerners think we still don't have, such as water supplies and sewage systems. Sadly, all this good work was cancelled out when they founded London, providing a future breeding ground for countless unbearable toffs and cockneys. Plus, they had the bastard cheek to name the North 'Britannia Inferior' and the South 'Britannia Superior'. Apparently these names had more to do with proximity to Rome than comparative quality, which must have been quite hard to explain while you were getting your Roman arse kicked.

With their love of sport, music and combat, the Romans left a lasting impact on the culture of the North. And with their love of poncing around in dresses and drinking wine, they also left a lasting impact on the culture of the South.

The Romans pulled out of Britain at the beginning of the fifth century, and in their place came migrants from Germany and Denmark including the Angles, Saxons and Jutes. It was to prove the most devastating impact the Germans would have on the North until they bombed Stan Boardman's chippy a few centuries later. The entire country descended into the Dark Ages where violence, poverty and disease were rife and learning and culture fell into decline. It was pretty much what Boris Johnson imagines Leeds to be like.

## Viking apekatt

The next invaders were the Vikings in the ninth century, and they were probably the most significant for the development of the North–South divide. Beginning with the attack on Lindisfarne Monastery in AD 793 and continuing with raids on both east and west coasts, the Vikings came over in such numbers that Alfred the Great was forced to make a deal with them, splitting the country into Danelaw in the North and Mercia and Wessex in the South.

Although the Danelaw was eventually brought back under English control, Scandinavian influences remained in the North. So as well as place names ending in words like 'thwaite', which means 'meadow', 'by', which means 'farm', and 'thorpe', which means 'village', the genetic influence of the Vikings can still be seen in the North today.

Vikings, like northerners, were good at fighting. Vikings, like northerners, loved to dress up in colourful clothing and believed that wearing loads of jewellery made you look like a badass player. And Vikings, like northerners, had dodgy facial hair.

## Le singe Normand to the modern Northern Monkey

Then in 1066 came the Battle of Hastings and the Norman Conquest of Britain, which basically involved the French ruling class swanning over and subjugating everyone. Naturally, with their love of French wine, French cheese and French cinema, southerners rolled over easily. As soon as King Harold got an arrow in his eye, they started sucking up to new boss William the Conqueror. But the North put up a stronger defence, with notable rebellions in Durham and York. William's response, the infamous 'Harrying of the North', was to lay waste to the entire region. He massacred thousands, burnt villages and destroyed food stocks so that any survivors would starve. It was a policy for dealing with the region that Margaret Thatcher would borrow from heavily in the eighties. William's extreme policies were effective. The North came under Norman control and once again the Northern Monkey species was fundamentally changed.

The species continues to evolve today, but whatever our differences, we'll always be bound together by the beliefs we share – that talking to strangers doesn't mean you're mad, that Greggs is a better lunch destination than Pret A Manger and that any pub that charges more than three quid a pint is going to be full of wankers.

# Ten Differences Between Northerners and Southerners

Ask a southerner what the main differences between the North and the South are and they'll scoff that they've got gas and electricity, and don't have to use the kettle to fill up the bath (or barth, as they call it). But you should be aware of a few genuine differences between the inhabitants of these two regions.

## Northerners are friendlier

Walk into a shop and greet the person behind the counter in the North and they'll greet you back. Walk into a shop in the South and greet the shopkeeper and they'll tell you to buy something or fuck off.

Try to turn out of a side road in the North and a fellow motorist will stop, give you a thumbs-up and let you onto the road. Try to turn out of a side road in the South and you're likely to get a different hand gesture altogether.

The simple truth is that northerners are nicer. We say 'thank you driver' as we step off the bus. We make small talk in queues. We even, God forbid, chat to people who live on the same street as us.

All of which might seem implausible to southerners who, despite being shoved into close physical proximity in their overcrowded bit of the island, act as if everyone around them is a hologram.

It makes you wonder why hermits bother to find caves when they want to escape from human contact. If they really want to achieve complete isolation, the best thing they can do is sit on a crowded rush hour tube and try and start a conversation.

## Northerners can hold their drink

A pub in Newcastle once offered customers free use of thetoilets with every five pints of lager they bought. Needless to say, none of their patrons were soft enough to take them up on the offer, with most locals waiting until at least the following Tuesday to strain their greens.

## Northerners actually spend some of their waking hours outside of work

I know this sounds crazy, but in the North it's actually possible to hold down a job by putting in less than seventy hours a week. In fact there are even some workplaces that are deserted at 5 p.m. because everyone's gone home or down the pub. I know that anyone down South who was caught suggesting such a worker's uprising would be given a formal warning, but that's what happens.

## Northerners can pop home after work before going out for the night

Many northerners live so near to where they work they can go home and get ready before going out on weeknights. Imagine that, commuters in the South East. It means you don't have to wear dull office clothes in the pub or drag huge laptop bags around. You can even have a shower and roll on some deodorant before going out. So contrary to the stereotype that we only use baths to store coal or ride down hillsides in, most northerners are actually cleaner than their sweaty southern counterparts.

## Northerners have a bit more space around them
We don't have to cram ourselves into trains and buses so tightly that we catch diseases off each other. We don't have to go home to wardrobes that estate agents have sold to us as 'luxury compact apartments'. And we can go for a walk in a park that's slightly less crowded than Harrods on the first day of the January sales. And the irony, of course, is that northerners are nicer, so you don't even *want* to be further away from them.

## Northerners can get to the countryside easily
A day trip to the countryside from London really does take up an entire day. Wherever you are in the North, you can pop out for a country stroll and be back within a couple of hours. And we get proper countryside up here too, rather than the slightly less built-up industrial estates that count as countryside down South.

## Northerners offer their seats to pregnant women
If a pregnant woman gets on a bus or train in the North, it's likely that someone nice will give up their seat so she can sit down. If a pregnant women gets on a bus or train in the

South, everyone will bury their heads deeper into their broadsheets, pretend they haven't seen her and mutter to themselves, 'Well, she's made her own bed and now she's got to facking well lie in it.'

## Northerners are harder

It's a proven scientific fact that northerners are harder than southerners. Well, there's no actual evidence, but come on. Just look at them. The hardest men in the entire south, such as Vinnie Jones and Ross Kemp, could still be beaten by the weakest, most malnourished child from the North. Even the words they use to describe hard people like 'naughty', 'handy' and 'tasty' sound soft.

## Northerners can actually do something useful

Ever tried to hire a plumber, a decorator or an electrician down South? Chances are they'll turn up, make a mess and then get called away on an 'urgent job' for a few weeks, only to hit you with a bill that's five times the estimate when they finish months later. The reason they behave like this is because they can. They enjoy their position of power because most southerners lack basic practical skills. They're perfectly capable when it comes to wanging on in meetings. But when it comes to useful stuff they can't find their arse with both hands.

Let's just take comfort from the notion that in the barbaric dark age we'll all be plunged back into with the coming global apocalypse, we northerners can use our manual skills to build shelters and hunt for food while southerners huddle around the last remaining Nobo board and hold a brainstorming session about how to avoid starvation.

### The climate is warmer in the North

Admittedly, the statistics don't back me up on this one. But think about it. Northerners wear T-shirts or skimpy dresses all year round, while southerners run off crying to the big coat shop as soon as August is over. So it must be true.

# CURRENCY CONVERSION GUIDE

Although the money used in the North and in the South looks the same, there are in fact two totally separate currencies, with one north pound equal to roughly four south pounds. If you're planning a trip to the South, a good rule of thumb is to work out how much you think you'll need, then double it, then double it again, then sell all your possessions and shove the money into a wheelbarrow before heading south. Here are a few examples of how the currency of the South differs:

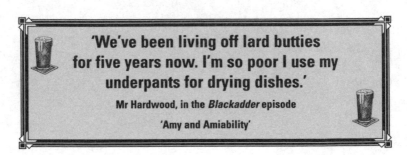

**'We've been living off lard butties for five years now. I'm so poor I use my underpants for drying dishes.'**

**Mr Hardwood, in the *Blackadder* episode**

**'Amy and Amiability'**

| NORTHERN NAME | NORTHERN PRICE | SOUTHERN NAME | SOUTHERN PRICE |
|---|---|---|---|
| Crisps | 35p | Hand-cut vegetable shavings | £1.45 |
| Cheese and onion butty | £1.25 | Ciabatta with caramelized onion and parmesan | £4.95 |
| Bus ticket | £1.20 | Tube ticket | £4.00 |
| Ticket for the pictures | £5.00 | Ticket for the cinema | £15.00 |
| Pint of bitter | £1.85 | Imported bottle of specialist lager from our extensive menu | £4.35 |
| Cup of tea | 60p | Chai latte | £2.85 |
| Gig ticket | £15 | Concert ticket | £45 |
| Pie | £1.20 | Filo parcel | £8.95 |
| Egg custard | 50p | Pastel de nata | £1.85 |
| Ham and cheese toastie | £1.25 | Chorizo and feta panini | £5.95 |
| Chicken nuggets and chips | £1.99 | Chicken goujons and pommes frites | £7.95 |

# THE MOST NORTHERN PLACES

**There's more to visiting the North than going on a walking holiday in the Lake District. Here are a few places that aren't to be missed on the itinerary of anyone looking for a truly northern experience.**

## Manchester

A major city in the Industrial Revolution, Manchester was once the international centre of textile manufacture. By the eighties, the city had fallen so far into decline that local bands Joy Division and The Smiths were regarded as too positive and upbeat. But Manchester's back now, having undergone more regeneration than a timelord in recent years.

Some of this occurred as a result of an IRA bomb that went off in 1996, which caused no fatalities but led to the construction of several new shopping complexes. So as far as terrorist attacks go, it was right up there with adding a pleasant water feature to Piccadilly Gardens.

Further regeneration occurred when Manchester successfully hosted the Commonwealth Games in 2002, which makes you wonder if it should be them and not London hosting the 2012 Olympics. After all, they've already got the tracksuits, and the locals would do well in the shooting if they could only pass the drugs tests.

> **'I would like to live in Manchester, England. The transition between Manchester and death would be unnoticeable.'**
>
> Mark Twain, American writer (1835–1910)

## Wakefield

Sod Dove Cottage. If you really want to know what the North is like, go to Wakefield and do the Westgate run, a pub crawl that involves going for a pint in each of the fifteen pubs that line Westgate Road. And if you're visiting from the South, the locals might even make an allowance and let you go to the toilet before you've completed it. You'll be in for a wonderfully authentic Yorkshire Saturday night, which will be a cross between *Saving Private Ryan* and a Black Lace video. It's all a bit less wonderful on a Sunday morning, when the entire town is covered with kebabs and multicoloured Bacardi Breezer vomit.

## Haworth

This is the Yorkshire that Japanese and American tourists see – cobbled streets, steep moors and desperate attempts to associate everything with the Brontës, who lived in Haworth Parsonage. You can walk the Brontë trail, cross the Brontë bridge, visit the Brontë chair and, quite probably, park in the Brontë pay-and-display car park.

## York

Historic walled city that was founded by the Romans in AD 71. Although many feel that it suffers in comparison with the new version across the Atlantic, York has no reason to feel inferior. It's the city that sleeps very well thank you, and if you can make it there, you'll probably be able to achieve a similar level of success throughout the region.

York is also home to Jorvik Viking Centre. Given the fearsome reputation of the Vikings, you'd expect this attraction to be a cross between the corkscrew at Alton Towers, a Slipknot mosh pit and a cheese dream. In fact it sets out to dispel the myth that the Vikings were ruthless pillagers by displaying lifeless mannequins in old-fashioned clothes going about their mundane business of working and shopping. And if you want to see that, it's much cheaper just to go to Barnsley.

## Liverpool

No fan of The Fabs would want to miss Liverpool, and the chance to see the Cavern, Penny Lane and Strawberry Fields. Although there were only four of them, the Beatles were close and personal friends with over 90 per cent of the population of Liverpool, and any Scousers in their swinging sixties will be happy to share stories and answer your questions about the Beatles. Unless your question is 'If Liverpool's so great, why did they move to London as soon as they became successful like every other celebrity from here?'

## Hull

Once voted the crappest town in Britain, Hull would come a very long way down anyone's list of places to visit in the UK. And, admittedly, it's not the prettiest town in the world, but that's the fault of the Luftwaffe and sixties town planners rather than the residents. At any rate, Robinson Crusoe sails from Hull and spends much of the novel wishing he'd never left it, so it must be nicer than a tropical desert island.

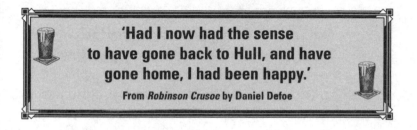

'Had I now had the sense
to have gone back to Hull, and have
gone home, I had been happy.'

From *Robinson Crusoe* by Daniel Defoe

## Newcastle

It seems strange that, while the West Yorkshire tourist board invites us to 'visit Brontë country', the Newcastle tourist board has been so slow to adopt 'visit *Viz* country' as its slogan. But this surely is the great draw of the Bigg Market on a Saturday night. Look, there are the Fat Slags on the prowl on for a lush bloke so they can get tops and fingers in a car park. And over there we can see Sid the Sexist telling a woman to sit on his face so he can guess her weight. And who's this approaching now? Why, it's Biffa Bacon, coming over to give us a fucking good kicking.

## Pity Me

Small village in County Durham, which is notable for having the dourest place name in the North, unless there's a village called 'Can't Be Arsed' or 'It's Still Ages Until Giro Day'. The origin of the name isn't certain, but it probably refers to a local boggy waste-ground called Pithead Mere, rather than the fact that the locals all sit around listening to Morrissey and complaining.

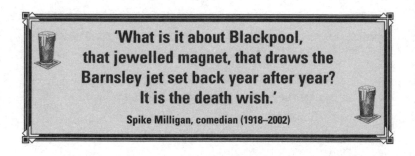

'What is it about Blackpool, that jewelled magnet, that draws the Barnsley jet set back year after year? It is the death wish.'

Spike Milligan, comedian (1918–2002)

## Blackpool

A place so gleefully downmarket it has vending machines for novelty thongs. At the Pleasure Beach you can see a scary mechanical clown, some scary skeletons riding bikes on the ghost train, a scary rollercoaster called the Pepsi Max Big One and a scary hen party wearing L-plates. If anyone from Islington ever visited, they'd have to spend a month in the National Gallery listening to a string quartet just to recover.

## Nob End

Pity Me isn't quite the best place name in the North, though, as there's actually an area near Bolton called Nob End. Disappointingly, it's not the hometown of Vernon Kaye, but a small village on the Manchester, Bolton and Bury Canal, and a waste of comedy name. Maybe we should try and get it twinned with Hoxton.

### ALREET PET

A 2007 study by the veterinary charity PDSA revealed that southerners are more likely to own cats, whereas northerners are more likely to own dogs. And believe it or not, this applies to all breeds of dog and not just whippets.

It's not too hard to imagine why northerners identify so strongly with friendly, loyal canines while southerners feel they have more in common with fickle, arrogant felines. Although given the amount of space most southerners have got in their houses, I'm surprised goldfish or Tamagotchi don't top their list of favourite pets.

# A FEW DIFFERENT SPECIES OF NORTHERN MONKEY

Although the term 'Northern Monkey' is bandied about as though there's no particular difference between anywhere in the North, the truth is that there are many different kinds of monkey to be found here. So make your southern colleagues/friends/neighbours study the following; if they're going to call us names, they can at least make them accurate ones.

## Geordies (Newcastle)

This term derives from the name 'George', but no one seems to know the identity of the George in question. It could refer to the region's support for George II during the Jacobite Rebellion in the eighteenth century. It could refer to the safety lamps designed by George Stephenson worn by miners in the nineteenth century. Or it might simply be that the name was so popular in the region that it became a nickname for all its inhabitants, in much the same way that 'Bruce' means Australian, 'Sharon' or 'Tracy' means Essex girl, 'Nathan' means twat from Hoxton and 'Tarquin' means twat from Kensington.

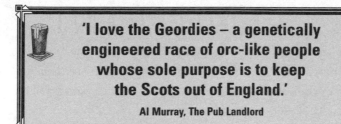

'I love the Geordies – a genetically
engineered race of orc-like people
whose sole purpose is to keep
the Scots out of England.'

**Al Murray, The Pub Landlord**

## Mackems (Sunderland)

This term seems to have its roots in shipbuilding, with the most popular theory being that it derives from 'we mack'em and ye tack'em', i.e. 'we make the ships and you take the ships'. Sadly they're more likely to 'mack' cold calls on Wearside these days, which nobody wants to 'tack'.

## Monkey-hangers (Hartlepool)

Nothing to do with the term Northern Monkey, this is in fact a reference to the myth that the people of Hartlepool hung a shipwrecked monkey during the Napoleonic Wars because they believed it to be a French spy. Although the story is now reckoned to be apocryphal, the term is still used to affectionately chide Hartlepudlians today, as is the football chant 'Tie a yellow gibbon round the old oak tree'.

## Tykes (Yorkshire)

'Tyke' is a term that's derived from an Old Norse word and lives on as a reminder of the region's Viking influence. It sounds quaint now, and many choose to use a more cutting-edge alternative such as 'Yorkshire Pudding'.

## Codhead (Hull, Whitby or Grimsby)

This nickname is given to people from towns such as Hull and Grimsby that traditionally had busy fishing industries, on the grounds that anyone who comes from these towns smells like a fish. Just for the record, I've been to Hull and it doesn't smell of fish. It smells of charity shops.

## Smoggies (Middlesbrough)

A nickname derived from the smoke of heavy industry that used to hang over Middlesbrough. Much of this industrial pollution has now gone, of course, and if you notice a thick smog hanging over the town now, it's probably because all the smokers have been forced to stand outside the pubs.

## Woollybacks (Warrington, Wigan, Widnes, Runcorn or St Helens)

A term used by Scousers to refer to the inhabitants of neighbouring towns. The word was probably first used to refer to dockyard workers who would carry wool onto the ships, and therefore seemed to have woolly backs. Some Liverpudlians believe that the word is actually a sheep-shagging reference, but this doesn't really make sense. Of all the many things that you should worry about if you ever decide to have sex with a sheep, surely getting wool on your back would be the least of them?

## Mancs (Manchester)

Those wishing to insult Mancunians have never got much more inventive than omitting a few letters from the word. It alliterates nicely with the word 'monkey', though, to create the popular insult 'Manc Monkey'. Which is a rather apt insult given that thousands of Mancunians, such as Liam Gallagher and Ian Brown, think that affecting a simian walk makes you look hard rather than ridiculous.

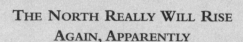

### THE NORTH REALLY WILL RISE AGAIN, APPARENTLY

In May 2009, HSBC published a report about the future of business that predicted that the traditional North–South divide would be turned on its head over the next twenty years, with northern 'super cities' like Leeds, Liverpool and Newcastle becoming more prosperous than their southern rivals. If you're reading this book in a charity shop in the future, I hope that the report turned out to be true and we're the ones who get to make jokes about 'thieving Southern monkeys' when something goes missing at work. At least it will let us carry on the great northern tradition of complaining about how much tougher we had it when we were kids.

## Clayheads (Stoke on Trent)

A term used to refer to inhabitants of those Staffordshire towns that like to refer to themselves as 'the Potteries' because it sounds more picturesque than 'the factories that used to be involved in ceramics manufacture'. 'Potheads' would make a much cooler name for people who inhabit these towns if it wasn't already taken by people who inhabit their parents' spare rooms and listen to Pink Floyd.

## Scousers (Liverpool)

This popular slang term derives from 'lobscouse', a meat stew that was originally eaten by sailors and became popular in Liverpool. So Liverpudlians are named after their favourite food. By which token, they should really be called 'Icelanders' now, but that's already taken.

# THE NORTHERN MONKEY SURVIVAL GUIDE TO LONDON

'When a man is tired of London,
he is tired of life.'

Samuel Johnson, author and lexicographer (1709–1784)

Dr Johnson's famous quotation serves as a mantra for the city's seven million inhabitants, who desperately want to convince themselves that they enjoy travelling to work in conditions that would get animal rights campaigners in a huff if they involved cattle rather than people. Tired of life just because you're tired of that overpriced shithole? My, as I believe Jim Royle said, arse.

But there will no doubt come a time when you'll have to visit our great capital. Perhaps you'll be stumbling around Wembley with a scarf and a novelty wig. Perhaps you'll be off to the Tate Modern to look at half a cow. Perhaps you'll be watching a reality TV star in a West End musical. Whatever the reason, it's important that you understand the strange customs of the place before you arrive.

## Before you go

First, you'll need to work out what to pack. Ask a Southern Jessie and they'll probably tell you to pack shorts, sun tan lotion and a fan to help you cope with their sweltering climate. This is a sad southern delusion. You'll actually find that the weather isn't massively different. At any rate, you shouldn't waste the valuable packing space: simply find every spare bag and case in your house and stuff them full of cash, to prepare you for the extortionate prices you'll be paying down there.

## Getting there

You'll start to notice southern prices coming into effect the moment you step into your local station and ask for a ticket. At first it might seem odd that the price the clerk is asking for is more than a return air ticket to Barcelona. But in truth he's only preparing you for the kind of price-hike you'll encounter in the big smoke. For example, it was recently calculated that travelling by tube from Piccadilly Circus to Leicester Square is more expensive for the distance covered than a luxury trip on the Orient Express. And instead of the Swiss Alps, you'll be looking at the jowls of sweaty commuters.

Not that you should be getting on the tube for such a short distance, of course. The tube map is deliberately designed to make places in London look much further apart than they really are. That way Londoners can treat you like a backward yokel just because you changed at Holborn and Tottenham Court Road when going from Russell Square to Goodge Street.

## Around town

As you walk around the capital, don't worry if you detect a strange smell in the air. It's just the overbearing stench of self-importance. It's generally pretty harmless, but if you hear the words 'village-y vibe', someone in the media using the words 'brave' or 'edgy', or a child named after the South American mountain it was conceived on, you might find yourself suffering from nausea. The best thing to do is go straight back up North again and drink a pint with a proper head on it until the horror goes away.

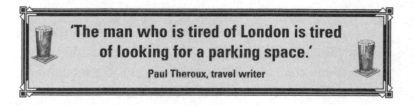

'The man who is tired of London is tired of looking for a parking space.'

Paul Theroux, travel writer

## Road safety

After you've fought your way along the pavement, skilfully manoeuvring around the homeless people, free newspaper vendors and students in fluorescent tabards trying to sign you up for direct debit charity donations, you might want to cross the road. But, for your own safety, you should be aware of a few differences you'll encounter when crossing the road in London. You should take particular care when approaching a zebra crossing. Down South, the cars won't automatically stop for you as you walk across. You'll have to wait for a driver to do you the favour of obeying the law, letting you cross and not killing you.

Even pelican crossings in London can be difficult. Many of

them resemble the starting grid of a race to find out which motorbike courier can kill you first. As you wait for the little man to turn green, your path may be blocked by a bendy bus, which is stuck halfway over the crossing, forcing you to walk a few miles around it just to get to other side of the street.

On the whole, you should be extra vigilant on London roads even if they seem safe. Most drivers of BMWs and Chelsea tractors are so rich they can afford to have your death hushed up if they kill you, so avoiding cars is pretty much your problem.

## Emergency services

If you do have the misfortune to get run over, don't bother calling an ambulance. Workers like ambulance drivers and nurses can't afford to live in London because it's so expensive. You could drag yourself to the nearest hospital and wait in A&E, but it's probably quicker to get the train home and get treated there.

## Lost?

If you're lost, don't bother stopping anyone to ask for directions. Southerners will probably tell you where to go, but not in the sense you were hoping for.

## Local cuisine

At some point on your trip, you'll need to find somewhere to eat. You might be tempted to try a famous London restaurant such as The Ivy, but unless you're a celebrity (and I mean a proper celebrity – being an *X Factor* audition freak doesn't count), you'll probably find that they're mysteriously full. So you'll have to take your chances at one of London's budget options. As long as you avoid the Albanian hotdog stands outside all major tourist attractions, and the stalls selling rancid slices of pizza for five quid, your stomach should be safe. Just don't ask for scraps, a barm cake or a steak pudding and they should be able to understand you.

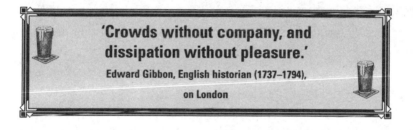

**'Crowds without company, and dissipation without pleasure.'**

Edward Gibbon, English historian (1737–1794),

on London

## Nightlife

After you've eaten, you'll probably be after a swift pint, so you'll be off to seek out a pub. This can be confusing at first, as most boozers in London have names like 'Thirst', 'Truth' and 'Remix' rather than 'The Red Lion' or 'Scunthorpe Working Men's Club'. And it's often hard to tell if you've found a pub, hairdressers or art gallery, because they all have similarly pretentious names.

When you've located a pub, don't bother looking at the taps to see what beers they have. Instead, you should ask for the 'bar menu' and you'll be presented with a list of bottled Eastern European lagers that start from as little as £5. You'll also notice that the bar staff will present your change and receipt on a little silver tray, as though they're expecting a tip for removing the bottle top. Obviously, with the drinks being so cheap, you shouldn't expect to be able to actually sit down. Of course not. That would be ridiculous. In fact, you'll be lucky most nights if you are able to stand inside. Most of the time you'll be expected to drink on the pavement outside like an alcoholic tramp.

## Having a piss

After you've had about twenty bottles of weak lager, you'll be ready for your first piss of the night. Sadly, this can also be rather complicated, as toilets in southern pubs tend to have indecipherable symbols on the doors rather than the words 'male' and 'female'. And even if you do work it out, you'll probably have to wait ages, as there will be far too few cubicles, and most of them will be locked, with strange chopping and snorting noises coming from inside.

## Getting away from it all

If you've been in London for a while, you'll start to notice that when you blow your nose, the snot comes out black instead of green. You might well be alarmed by this, and want to take a break in the countryside near London. Sadly, there isn't any. Although London does have some green spaces such as Hampstead Heath and Clapham Common, they're so crowded with cottaging Tory MPs and eighties pop stars that they don't provide much respite from the bustle of the city. And as for the rest of the South East, it's been concreted over for a series of identical, stifling commuter towns that aren't even worth looking at through a train window. And even if you do make it out of the suburban sprawl you won't find proper countryside anyway. Unlike their fizzy lager, southerners prefer their countryside flat. And as with the booze, you'll have to wait until you get back up North to enjoy it.

## Arriving home

You'll no doubt be relieved to get back up North and try to forget your whole experience. But be careful not to mention to your friends that you're been to the capital or everything you do or say will be taken as evidence that you've gone 'all posh' since you went to 'that London'.

# THE TEN SMUGGEST AREAS TO LIVE IN LONDON

It's not just the centre of London you should avoid. Every single part of the place is unbearable in its own unique way. If you have to move down there because of work, this handy guide should help you decide that commuting from the North is the best option.

### Shoreditch
The only place in the country where they need micro scooter lanes on the roads, Shoreditch is considered wanky even by Londoners. Everyone there has a trendy asymmetrical haircut, the latest iPhone and a job in 'new media' that doesn't seem to involve much except listening to obscure hip hop on Spotify.

### The City
As well as housing London's financial district, The City also contains the famous 'Bow bells' of St Mary-le-Bow church off Cheapside. It's often said that anyone born within earshot of the bells is a proper cockney. Coincidentally, it's also true that anyone born within earshot of cockneys is a proper bell.

## Clapham

When Russian billionaires priced all the Tarquins and Jemimas out of Kensington, everyone wondered where they would go next, desperately hoping that idiots with pashminas and double-barrelled names wouldn't move in next to them. To the horror of gnarly South Londoners, they settled in Clapham, creating a toff colony and inspiring greedy landlords to chop Victorian terraces into studio flats smaller than iPod Shuffles.

## Chelsea

If you think you hate the team, wait until you see the place. This part of South West London is so infested with unbearable Rahs, Yahs and Hooray Henrys, that the area's main square has given its name to the female of the species, Sloanes.

## Camden Town

Are you the kind of person who sits at the Glastonbury stone circle and says, 'I wish we could all just live here forever, man'? If so, Camden could be the place for you. You'll be able to buy tie-dye T-shirts, massive Doc Martens, indie vinyl and Oxo cubes from drug dealers all year round.

## Islington

A place so riddled with journalists, producers, publishers, admen and designers that just visiting should earn you a media studies GCSE. Islington is based around an interminable high street of restaurants and cafes filled with people in thick-rimmed glasses making quotation marks with their fingers as they talk about their edgy new projects.

## Primrose Hill

This North London suburb is undoubtedly the celebrity capital of the UK. And if you think seeing someone who's shorter than they look on telly doing their shopping is worth the extortionate property prices, I'm sure there are plenty of estate agents who would love to meet you.

## Richmond

Eight miles west of London, with a huge park and several riverside pubs, Richmond is the kind of place that makes Londoners say, 'It's brilliant, you don't even feel like you're in London at all', before realizing that they've let slip the truth that they don't really like their city.

## Hampstead

Posh North London suburb that features some of the most expensive properties in the world. Even in a recession you wouldn't get much change from £50 million if you wanted to buy a house on Bishops Avenue. And what would you get for it? Gold post boxes? Chandelier street lamps? Supermodel lollipop ladies? Nope, just a deserted street of mansions owned by Saudi and Russian billionaires who visit them once or twice a year. There isn't even a decent chippy.

## Peckham

The kind of place a letting agent will tell you to check out when you move down to London and tell them how much you'd like to spend on rent. They'll call it 'vibrant'. You'll go there and see that it's actually vibrantly terrifying. And the worst thing is, rent is still more expensive here than in a nice part of a northern city.

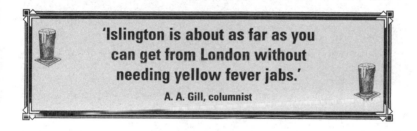

'Islington is about as far as you can get from London without needing yellow fever jabs.'

A. A. Gill, columnist

# TEN SOUTHERN PLACES TO AVOID

While it might be understandable that you'll have to go to Heathrow, Gatwick or Wembley at some point, there's no reason you should ever have to visit the rest of the South. Still, here's a selection of southern places you might not be able to avoid.

### Luton/Croydon/Watford etc.

Interchangeable satellite towns that can match anywhere in the North for dullness, but still charge you exorbitant southern prices. They've all got a Cash Converters, they've all got precincts littered with empty Kansas Fried Chicken boxes and they're all full of mouth-breathers who look like they're waiting to appear on *The Jeremy Kyle Show*.

### Oxford

Although known for its quadrangles, dreaming spires and future Tory MPs, Oxford is surrounded by rough estates, the inhabitants of which descend on the town centre on Saturday night, making it seem as if the portal from *His Dark Materials* has opened and the spectres have descended.

### Essex

Any southerners who feel they've got the right to be snobbish about the North should be forced to go to Romford, Chelmsford or any of those Essex towns that you can catch chlamydia from just from passing through on the train. Each one is a nightmarish tableau of vomit, white jeans and tit mooning that looks like something Hieronymus Bosch would dream up after too many Bacardi Breezers. After a dose of this hellishness, the Bigg Market will feel like wine and canapés at the Tate.

## Norfolk
The three-fingered residents might seem friendlier than most southerners, but this is only because their limited gene pool makes it hard for them to understand that they haven't met you before. Asking them for even the simplest directions is likely to get them running off to their mother-sister or father-brother for help.

## The West Country
If you like cream teas, pasties and Liberal Democrats, you might consider visiting Cornwall, Devon, Dorset or Somerset. Admittedly, the region does have its pleasantly quaint parts, but the novelty of visiting places where even the people wearing suits talk like hobbits and pirates soon wears off, so the long journey from the North isn't really worth it.

## The Cotswolds
Tourism is an important industry here, so you'll probably find the people to be friendly in a self-interested kind of way. But visit in a year when the crops have failed, and you'll be burned in a huge wicker effigy as a sacrifice to the gods of the fields.

## Bristol

It is surely no compliment to a city when a production company chooses it as the venue for the thick person's version of *Who Wants To Be A Millionaire?* In *Deal or No Deal*, a contestant will win the amount of money inside a box that's chosen at random. However, to pad the running time out to forty-five minutes, the contestants have to be so stupid that they believe the order they eliminate the boxes in will affect the result, and that employing the right tactics will increase their final winnings. And where did Endemol go to find such oxygen thieves? Bristol, that's where.

## Dover

Traditionally, Dover was the first place in England that the French used to experience. No wonder they think we're all a bit backwards. Nowadays, of course, the Eurostar plonks them right in the middle of King's Cross, so the first English people they see are drug dealers, alcoholics and ladyboys. Grim, perhaps, but they still manage to make a better first impression than the inhabitants of Dover used to do.

## Milton Keynes

If you had the chance to create a completely new town, what would you want it to be like? Paris? Tokyo? Cloud City from *The Empire Strikes Back*? Southerners had a chance in the sixties and they decided to make theirs look like a massive B&Q car park. If they had their way, they'd make all towns exactly like this too: a hellish maze of roundabouts, industrial estates and broken water features.

## Brighton

Less than an hour away from the capital, Brighton is the place Londoners go to 'get away from it all'. Although quite how fannying around exactly the same chain restaurants and listening to exactly the same media wankers yap into their iPhones counts as getting away from it all, I don't know. There's a pebble beach, I suppose, but when the weather's halfway decent it gets more crowded than the Northern Line during rush hour. Brighton? London-by-Sea, more like.

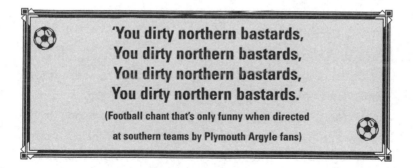

'You dirty northern bastards,
You dirty northern bastards,
You dirty northern bastards,
You dirty northern bastards.'

(Football chant that's only funny when directed
at southern teams by Plymouth Argyle fans)

# TIPS FOR SOUTHERNERS HEADING TO THE NORTH

If you're a Southern Jessie and you're intrigued by the rich culture of the North, you might be considering a visit. It's certainly highly recommended, but there are a few points of etiquette that should help make your trip both hassle-free and fucking-good-kicking-in-the-pub-car-park-free.

### What to take

When packing, try not to be panicked into bringing the kind of clothes that are usually brought on an Arctic expedition. While some places in the North will have slightly lower temperatures than you're used to, the difference won't be as huge as you expect, and you'll only give yourself away as a tourist if you wear too many layers. You'll have a better experience of the region if you don't trumpet your southern identity, so you should also leave your sarong, cravat, manbag and guyliner at home. On the other hand, don't go so far with your attempts to blend in that you wear a flat cap and braces and smear your face with coal soot.

## Local customs

As soon as you get off the train in the North, you might notice that people you don't know are making small talk or even addressing you as 'love'. Don't be alarmed by this: it doesn't necessarily mean they're trying to rob you. They might just be nice. If someone does start a conversation with you, try to avoid the topics of how rich you are, and how much cheaper everything is in the North. If you bray on about such topics for too long you might find the legendary friendliness of northerners somewhat lacking.

If you have to get on a bus or some other form of public transport, remember that there's no need to automatically press your face into the armpits of a stranger. Unlike in the South, there will probably be enough room for you to have a seat all to yourself.

## Recreation

At some point on your visit, you'll probably want to enjoy the traditional northern pastime of getting pissed. And being a soft southern shite, you won't find this too difficult. You should be able to tell immediately if you've found somewhere that's welcoming to non-locals. If the music pauses, a group of fat blokes in the corner stops playing darts and the bar staff spit on the ground when they see you, it probably isn't. At any rate, you should be able to find a pub that you feel comfortable in soon enough, and you might even find one that serves those fizzy lagers you love so much. However, please make an effort to respect local culture and refrain from ordering halves if you're male. And for pity's sake don't ask for a lager top. You've got more chance of finding the letters 'h' and 'e' in the definite article than lime cordial in lager in most northern pubs.

## Amenities

After a few sips, you'll probably need the toilet, which is known in the North as 'the bog', 'the shitter' or 'the shithouse'. After you've relieved yourself, please observe local etiquette and avoid washing your hands. And, for God's sake, don't ask where the bidet is.

## Around town

By the time you've got to the end of your second pint, you'll probably be talking loudly and getting in the mood to move on to a local nightclub. Whichever town you're in, you'll be able to find a club called something like 'Monroez', 'Legendz', 'Destinyz', 'Elementz', 'Chaserz', 'Voltz' or 'Slagz' without much difficulty. If you're male, resist the temptation to rush onto the dance floor the moment your favourite song comes on. Especially if your favourite song is 'It's Raining Men' by The Weather Girls and the way you like to dance is by taking your T-shirt off and swinging it around your head. An important rule of etiquette in the North is that all the men must wait until all the women are already on the dance floor before they venture onto it. And even then, many of them prefer to stand on the edge of the dance floor and look on angrily as their girlfriends dance with other blokes.

## Emergency services

Soon you'll be reaching the end of that third pint and by now you'll probably be slurring your words and feeling quite aggressive. If you fancy starting a fight, you should find it pretty easy. Just stand in the queue at the kebab shop and talk loudly about money and you should have one on your hands soon enough. If that doesn't work, try approaching a hard bloke with a traditional fight-starting line such as, 'Are you looking at me or chewing a brick? Cos either way you'll end up getting your teeth broken.'

When you reach the local A&E department, why not conclude your night out with the traditional northern pastime of trying to pull the nurse? Although she's been on duty for the last twenty hours and you've got blood and sick caked down the front of your shirt, your sexual magnetism is likely to be so effective that she'll overlook these things and give in.

Whatever happens, you'll be able to return home with the ultimate souvenir of your trip to the North – a set of fresh stitches. Better than a Lake Windermere tea towel any day.

# THE NORTHERN MONKEY HALL OF FAME:
# THE GREATEST NORTHERNERS IN HISTORY

**If you think Kerry Katona and the bloke who does the voiceover for *Big Brother* have been the North's biggest contributions to the world, then familiarize yourself with these great Northern Monkeys.**

### William Wilberforce

Born in Hull in 1759, abolitionist leader Wilberforce later became Member of Parliament for Hull, a post that was more recently held by John Prescott. But while Wilberforce dedicated his life to fighting slavery, Prescott dedicated his to fighting people with mullets who threw eggs at him. So Wilberforce is the one who makes it onto the list.

### Emmeline Pankhurst

Most southerners think that letting your wife drink from a pint glass is about as far as feminism goes in the North. But the truth is that we pretty much invented it, with the rise of the women's suffrage movement in Manchester. The leader of the movement, Emmeline Pankhurst, was famed for her militant tactics, engaging in noisy protests that included deliberate property damage and window smashing. Emmeline's achievements are still commemorated by women in Manchester, who shout and break things every Saturday night to remind us all of the suffrage movement.

## The *Gawain* Poet

Nothing is really known about the author of Middle English poems *Pearl* and *Sir Gawain and the Green Knight*, but scholars of medieval dialect reckon he might have come from Lancashire or Cheshire. He probably didn't come from the Wirral, though, as he slags the area off in *Sir Gawain*:

> Into the wilderness of the Wirral, where few dwelled,
> To whom God or good-hearted man gave his love.

Although the poet doesn't go as far as accusing the people of the Wirral of stealing the hubcaps from his cart or telling him to 'calme downe, calme downe', it's interesting that even in the earliest examples of writing about the North, authors were happy to digress from the plot to have a go at Scousers.

## John Lennon

You don't have to be in Liverpool long (especially if you come via the airport) to be reminded that the greatest rock star of all time came from the city. There are some who believe Lennon's legendary status has been exaggerated by his tragic early death, and that if he'd lived long enough, he too would have recorded novelty tracks with cartoon frogs and married unpopular unipeds. But there's enough evidence on his last records to suggest that he'd have kept on banging out good stuff for decades to come. And in this age of digital music, it would be even easier to delete Yoko's contributions without ever having to listen to them.

## Stan Laurel

Ask anyone who the greatest ever northern comedian was, and they might say Eric Morecambe, Les Dawson or, if they find the word 'Germans' hilarious, Stan Boardman. But in fact the most famous comic ever to emerge from the region isn't really thought of as northern at all. Born in Ulverston in 1890, Laurel was half of the best-known double act in history. In recent years, colour footage has emerged revealing that Laurel was also a ginger, so he really did overcome the odds to become a Hollywood star.

## The Venerable Bede

In AD 731, Benedictine monk Bede completed *The Ecclesiastical History of the English People*, one of the most important original references on the history of the so-called 'Dark Ages'. Bede lived in the area that's now Sunderland, although, surprisingly, his book doesn't feature chapters on why everyone from Newcastle is a twat, and how easily Mackems can beat them in fights.

## Guy Fawkes

The Catholic revolutionary whose gunpowder plot was famously foiled on 5 November was originally from York. And while attempting to kill the King and blow up the Houses of Parliament can't really be condoned, it's probably time that the North stopped burning effigies of one of their own every year. Perhaps we should forgive Fawkes and start burning effigies of southerners like Boris Johnson and Jeffrey Archer instead.

## Captain James Cook

The explorer and cartographer was born in 1728 in Marton, which is now part of Middlesbrough. Although he didn't really discover Australia as is often supposed, he was the first European to visit its eastern coast. He was also the first person to map Newfoundland and he recorded the first circumnavigation of New Zealand. This disproves the notion that people from the North only ever leave the country to go on package tours to Greece that they found on Teletext, so they can spend two weeks moaning about how you can't get proper chips in the taverna.

## Rick Astley

The Newton-le-Willows pop star might seem like a strange addition to a list of the greatest people ever to emerge from the North, but if the vote was opened up to the public he would almost certainly win thanks to the Internet phenomenon of 'Rickrolling'. Initially, this involved posting a link that appears to be relevant to a particular topic, but actually takes you to the video for 'Never Gonna Give You Up'. Recently this has extended to voting for Astley in public polls, which lead to him being named as the Greatest Act Of All Time at the 2008 MTV music awards. As the meme gathers pace, expect him to win at the Oscars, the Ideal Home Exhibition and Crufts in the next couple of years.

As a tribute to Rickrolling, the rest of this book will consist of nothing but the lyrics of 'Together Forever' as soon as you click on **these words** with your finger.

## L. S. Lowry

Salford-born painter whose grim industrial landscapes were so popular in the first half of the twentieth century that many southerners still think they're an accurate depiction of the North. With their overcast skies, gloomy factories, bellowing chimneystacks, drab colours and stick-thin figures, Lowry's paintings managed to confirm every northern stereotype (except for the one about us eating all the pies).

In 2000, a complex called 'The Lowry' opened in Salford Quays, which contains theatres, art galleries and restaurants, but sadly no cotton factories where all visitors are forced to work eighteen-hour shifts wearing clogs.

# THE SOUTHERN HALL OF FAME

**If you need proof of how irredeemably shite the South is, take a look at the criminals, liars and bone idle aristocrats who pass for heroes down there.**

### Dick Van Dyke

Van Dyke's performance as Bert in *Mary Poppins* made him an icon in the South. Although some have mocked his attempt at a cockney accent, it was about as convincing as the legions of modern-day mockney students, violinists, TV chefs and gangster movie directors from the Home Counties who want to snare some street cred.

### Jeffrey Archer

If you think Boris Johnson is bad, look at the Tory they could have elected.

Archer embodies the southern quality of mercenary dishonesty so well that he would have made a very apt London mayor. Despite his conviction for perjury and subsequent imprisonment, Archer remains the most popular human being ever to have lived. That's not actually true, but I was given a brown paper bag full of money to say it.

## The Krays

Despite having spent most of their waking hours nailing people to floors, Ronnie and Reggie Kray are second only to the Queen in the affections of southerners. Cockneys of a certain age are likely to pretend that they knew the brothers and to absolve them on the grounds that they loved their mum and would always be nice and polite while kneecapping you.

Like most cockney criminals, the Krays have been portrayed on film by pop stars. Following the performances of Roger Daltrey in *McVicar* and Phil Collins in *Buster*, Gary and Martin Kemp from Spandau Ballet played the brothers in the 1989 biopic. Which all makes for a pretty unconvincing deterrent. You might be tempted to rob a bank or run a protection racket. But if you get caught, Simon Le Bon will play you in a crap film.

## The Queen

Posh bird who owns the best house in the whole of London, but still chooses to spend much of her time a few hundred miles north of it, which proves that the capital can't be all it's cracked up to be.

## Del Boy from *Only Fools and Horses*

As well as worshiping 'naughty naughty' gangsters like the Krays and 'Mad' Frankie Fraser, southerners also hold the patron saint of wide boy market-traders, Derek Trotter, close to their hearts. People who flog you fake antiques and DVDs that don't play? Gawd bless 'em, guv. Salt of the earth, they are.

## Richard Littlejohn

If you can't afford to get in a cab and listen to some ill-informed right-wing bilge, you could always go straight to the source and read Richard Littlejohn's column in the *Daily Mail*. People from all across the South can be heard tutting under their breath and muttering 'it's a diabolical liberty' as they plough through one of their hero's diatribes, which inevitably conclude with the catchphrase, 'You couldn't make it up!' Which is rather ironic given the paper in which they appear.

## Jack the Ripper

Serial killers aren't exclusive to the South, but it's only there that they are seen as opportunities for tourism. If you're ever in London and you feel like celebrating the unsolved murders of five prostitutes, you could choose from several Jack the Ripper museum exhibits or walking tours. But go up North, ask for the Myra Hindley gift shop or the Peter Sutcliffe heritage trail and you'll be run out of town.

## Disgusted of Tonbridge Wells

Generic term for petty Middle Englanders who pen complaint letters. And while this might seem like a pointless waste of time, you should remember that most of these people are so old that it's only their sense of moral outrage that's keeping them alive. In fact, the best thing we could do for them would be to build a community theatre workshop retreat for hoodies, asylum seekers and lesbians right in the middle of Tonbridge Wells and festoon it with a banner reading, 'We paid for this with taxpayers' money'.

## London cabbies

To qualify as a black cab driver, you need to be able to simultaneously demonstrate both a wide-ranging knowledge of London's streets and a wide-ranging ignorance of national politics. As the traffic moves so slowly down there, you'll have plenty of time to hear about how political correctness has gone mad and we're all going to hell in a handcart. That's not to say that all cab drivers in the North are mild-mannered *Guardian* readers who are happy to discuss European arthouse cinema with you as they give cyclists right of way, but in general they don't match their southern counterparts for misguided rage.

## Pearly kings and queens

Cockneys who dress in black costumes covered in mother-of-pearl buttons and were once regarded as figureheads for London's working-class communities. The tradition of covering yourself in shiny things to show how working class you are is still observed today by people who buy Elizabeth Duke jewellery from Argos.

# TEN JOKES THAT ARE ALWAYS MADE ABOUT NORTHERNERS

**If you ever venture down South, there's more than just the tropical climate you need to prepare for. You should also brace yourself for a series of 'hilarious' wisecracks that will be made at your expense.**

### We talk funny, like

Move to the South and it won't be long before someone does an impression of the way you talk. For most southerners this will involve a broad Yorkshire accent, as though everyone in the North, from Liverpool to Newcastle, talks like Geoffrey Boycott or John Prescott. More sophisticated office jokers might be able to differentiate between accents, and may even use the following repertory of stock northern phrases to showcase their impressions to hilarious effect.

> To someone from Liverpool: 'Dey don't do dat dere, do, doe dey, dough?' or 'Calm down, calm down', which is likely to have the exact opposite effect if you repeat it over and over again to a Scouser.

To someone from Manchester: 'Top one, nice one, sorted.'

To someone from Yorkshire: 'Ey up chuck' or 'Ee by gum'.

To someone from Newcastle: 'Why aye man' or 'Thou shalt have a fishy / On a little dishy / Thou shalt have a fishy / When de boot comes in.'

The temptation is to retort by mimicking a southern accent. This won't be especially difficult, as there are only three variations – toff, cockney and pirate. But I think we should resist sinking to their level. After all, we're the ones with normal accents and they're the ones who sound strange.

## We rob stuff

This seems to affect Scousers and Mancs in particular, but accusations of thievery have been labelled at all breeds of Northern Monkey at some point or another. This can range from snidey put-downs to public emails when something goes missing from someone's desk to 'classic' jokes such as . . .

*What do you call a Scouser in a suit?*
The accused.

Just to get this straight, southerners, we don't want any of your crappy stuff. In the unlikely event that we ever wanted some houmous, a Pilates mat and a 'world music' CD we'd be perfectly capable of buying them ourselves.

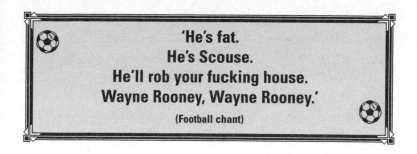

'He's fat.
He's Scouse.
He'll rob your fucking house.
Wayne Rooney, Wayne Rooney.'

(Football chant)

## We don't have jobs

Most southerners regard the whole of the North as an unemployment black spot, where redundant youths are forced to train kestrels or learn ballet just to claw back some self-respect. Again, Liverpool is the most likely target here, as when southern football fans chant 'Sign on, sign on with hope in your hearts' to the tune of 'You'll Never Walk Alone' or as in the following joke:

*Why did audiences scream so hard at The Beatles' concerts?*
The shock of seeing four Scousers working.

Thankfully, these jokes tend to become increasingly rare in recessions. While there are many obvious downsides to economic turmoil, there is at least the small comfort that southerners temporarily stop being smug about their overpaid banking and media jobs.

## We have rubbish jobs

Even when southerners can bring themselves to admit that we're employable, the joke tends to be that we're only good for menial jobs:

*What do you say to a northerner with a job?*
I'll have fries with that.

This is clearly nonsense. These days you're just as likely to find the job you're after on either side of the divide. Unless the job you're after is pearly king, purveyor of jellied eels and pies or criminal folk hero, in which case you'll still have to emigrate south. And good riddance to you.

### LONDON 0 HULL 4

When the Housemartins named their 1986 album *London 0 Hull 4*, it was intended as nothing more than a light-hearted dig at the beautiful South by singer Paul Heaton. But it went on to become a spookily accurate prediction when Hull beat the first four London teams they played upon promotion to the Premier League in 2008. If I was Paul Heaton I'd call my next album *Boris Johnson Will Die and I'll Win Ten Grand on a Scratchcard*.

## We wallow in tragedy

Perhaps the most offensive stereotype of all is that we go overboard with grief and sentimentality when a tragedy occurs. Again, the main culprit here is thought to be Liverpool, which has been labelled 'self-pity city' by cynics, and targeted in jokes like:

*What's the difference between a cow and a tragedy?*
A Scouser wouldn't know how to milk a cow.

This unfortunate stereotype came to prominence in 2005 when an unsigned leader article in the *Spectator* accused Liverpudlians of being 'hooked on grief' and wallowing in their 'victim status'. Unsurprisingly, these kind of accusations tend to be restricted to places such as anonymous think pieces in right-wing magazines rather than blurted out loud. Although if anyone ever did have the guts to say them in a pub in Toxteth they might end up experiencing tragedy first-hand.

## The blokes are all sheep-shaggers

The insult 'sheep-shaggers' and all its related jokes are used by southerners to describe anyone from the North, as if the entire top half of the country was so rural and deserted that we're all forced to get it on with sheep. The term is also used by northerners to refer to someone from a town that's slightly smaller than their own. It's a pretty safe rule of thumb that no matter how remote and unpopulated the hamlet you live in, there'll be somewhere smaller nearby that you regard as being full of lonely zoophiliacs.

Just for the record, southerners, we're not so desperate that we have to turn to the animal kingdom to get our rocks off. In fact, a 2006 survey by blob-mongers Durex revealed that people from Yorkshire have sex (with humans) more than anyone else in the UK, getting ten shags a year more than the national average. So if anything it's you lot who are more likely to be roaming the moors at night looking for a ewe with a pretty face.

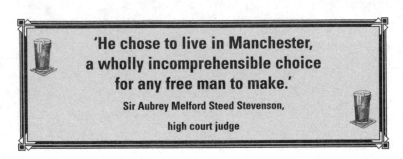

'He chose to live in Manchester, a wholly incomprehensible choice for any free man to make.'

Sir Aubrey Melford Steed Stevenson,

high court judge

## The girls are all slags

Confusingly, while southerners seem to believe that northern blokes are off shagging sheep, the women are incredibly promiscuous. Who with?

Take the following examples:

*How does a Geordie lass turn on the light after sex?*
She opens the car door.

Or:

*How do you define 'confusion'?*
Fathers' Day in Liverpool.

It might be true that people in the North enjoy more rompidedoodah (look it up in the Glossary, southerners), but that doesn't make us all tarts. In fact, come on, southern blokes: if you really believe that the girls up here are easy, why don't you prove it by coming up here and trying to pull? Something tells me that your charming, bumbling Hugh Grant act will get you as much action as halitosis.

## We're thick as pigshit

As with the long tradition of Irish jokes, some gags about the North exploit the notion that we're all a bit stupid up here. For example:

*Why wasn't Jesus born in (insert name of northern town here)?*
Because God couldn't find three wise men and a virgin.

Sadly, there will always be a type of ignorant southerner who equates a northern accent with stupidity, but it's not hard to turn these preconceptions to your advantage. After all, when you do make an intelligent contribution to a meeting or conversation it will shock the southerners so much that it will have a much greater impact.

So in fact the misconception is no bad thing. Unless you really are thick, of course, in which case stop trying to read a book and go and watch a Bernard Manning VHS instead.

## We don't leave a generation gap

Perhaps as a consequence of all the alleged promiscuity, northerners are also teased for having children too young:

*What do you call a 26-year-old Geordie lass?*
Grandma.

In fact, there is a genuine difference in the age that people have children in the North and the South. A 2008 study conducted by the Office for National Statistics revealed that women in the South are likely to have their first child in their early thirties, an average ten years later than new mums in the North. This is because it takes them an extra ten years to save up for private school fees, Gucci pushchairs, riding lessons and all the other things that will ensure the next generation of southerners are just as grating and insufferable as the current one.

## We live in poverty

After years of seeing men in grimy work clothes push bikes up hills to the sound of brass bands on TV, most southerners still think that the North is part of the Third World, as a sketch in Monty Python's *The Meaning of Life* had it. This is a joke that did the rounds in 1996:

> *Did you hear that the centre of Manchester has been destroyed by an IRA bomb?*
> It did £20 worth of damage.

This is another jibe that you only hear when the economy is doing well, and southerners have a pocketful of crisp tenners to wave at homeless people. When money gets tight for them, they go mysteriously quiet on the subject of how poor everyone else is.

### SOUTHERN SOFTIES

Statistics released by drug company Pfizer in 2002 revealed that the top five towns for Viagra sales were all south of the border. And, unsurprisingly, Londoners were the worst culprits. Which might help to explain why they regard northerners as promiscuous: for them, anyone who can get a bonk on without tablets counts as a male slag.

# THE NORTHERN MONKEY HALL OF FAME:
# PROFESSIONAL NORTHERNERS

They might not be the greatest people ever to come from the North, but they were certainly the most northern. In fact, if they were any more northern they'd be the Faroe Islands.

### The Macc Lads

Macclesfield might boast of being the birthplace of Joy Division legend Ian Curtis, but the sad truth is that lairy post-punks The Macc Lads painted a far more accurate picture of the Cheshire market town's youth culture. With songs like 'Miss Macclesfield', 'Eh Up! Let's Sup' and 'No Sheep Till Buxton', listening to the Macc Lads was like letting a man who's just drunk twenty pints of Boddingtons have a piss in your ear.

### Jim Bowen

Cheshire-born host of *Bullseye*, a quiz where the cash prize could be anything up to £15, which contestants could then gamble for some unsold Poundstretcher stock or Bully's special prize of a fitted kitchen. Watching Bowen and his mostly northern contestants get excited about such tat only helped to compound the misconception of the North as a wasteland of poverty-stricken darts fans brooding over what they could have won.

## Fred Trueman

Yorkshire cricket legend and host of *Indoor League*, a show that was broadcast from The Queen's Hotel in Leeds and featured traditional sports such as shove ha'penny, bar billiards and arm wrestling, stopping just short of whippet racing and giro fiddling. Greeting viewers with a curt 'Now then' and clutching a pint of bitter and a pipe, Trueman would present proper Yorkshire darts with 'no trebles, no fluky shots, just a hell of a lot of skill', as though playing darts on a trebles board was tantamount to skipping through a field of flowers wearing a pink dress.

## Peter Kay

If ever the North became an independent state, we wouldn't need to bother holding elections for prime minister. Peter Kay would automatically be sworn in, such is his popularity up here. With his observational gags about crap pop and dipping biscuits in your brew, Kay is the quintessential northerner in the way that Paul Hogan is the quintessential Aussie and Lord Voldemort is the quintessential southerner.

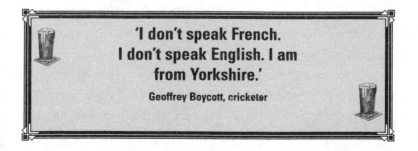

**'I don't speak French. I don't speak English. I am from Yorkshire.'**

Geoffrey Boycott, cricketer

## John Prescott

Worried that Labour's heartlands might not be able to relate to grinning Islingtonite Tony Blair, New Labour sought balance with the most northern politician it could find. It turned out that Prescott was so northern he even took to punching Welsh farmers in the face if they threw eggs at him. Sadly, though, he never went as far as beating up opposition members in the House of Commons car park at closing time.

## Fred Dibnah

Steeplejack from Bolton who became famous in the late seventies after a BBC documentary. He's best remembered for sequences in which he felled the chimneys of disused mills to the delight of local enthusiasts (no, seriously, chimney enthusiasts really existed in the days before PlayStations). Wearing a flat cap, covered in soot and banging on about how much grander life was in the Industrial Revolution, Dibnah was a living northern stereotype. He probably got home every night by pushing his bike up a hill to the strains of Dvořák's *New World* symphony.

## Brian Glover

Originally a wrestler and teacher, Glover turned to acting after he was cast as a bolshy Yorkshire PE teacher in Ken Loach's film *Kes*. After that he enjoyed a varied acting career, appearing as a bolshy Yorkshire villager in *American Werewolf in London* and a bolshy Yorkshire spaceman in *Alien 3*. He was also top of the list when a no-nonsense northern voiceover was required, and could be heard barking slogans like 'Tetley mek teabags mek tea' and 'Bread wi' nowt tekken out' as though we was standing on the top of Ilkley Moor and not sitting in a sound studio in Soho.

## Cilla Black

Former singer and telly host who is often cited as an example of a 'plastic Scouser': someone who barks on about how great Liverpool is and how you can leave your back door open all day, even though they got the hell out of there as soon as they made it. But this all seems rather unfair. Cilla has in fact been spending a lot of time in the 'Pool recently. Admittedly, though, this has been because she's been appearing in panto. And where does that mean your career is, boys and girls? Altogether now . . . Behind you!

## George Formby

Music hall and movie star from Wigan whose bawdy style influenced generations of northern comics. Though his humour might seem quaint by today's standards, Formby's double entendres were considered incredibly risqué in his day, and his song 'With My Little Stick of Blackpool Rock' was even banned by the BBC in 1937 on the grounds that he was comparing the popular confectionary item to his tallywhacker. It's hardly up there with telling a sitcom actor that you've fucked his granddaughter, but that's the kind of thing that used to offend people back then.

## Morrissey

In a poll held by The Lowry Centre in 2007, the Mancunian singer was voted the most northern male of all time, beating George Formby and Fred Dibnah.

And while the many references in his lyrics to kitchen-sink dramas such as *A Taste of Honey*, *Billy Liar* and *Saturday Night and Sunday Morning* root him firmly in the North, I'm not sure he's quite managed to out-northern the other two just yet. Only when he's sung a duet with Gracie Fields on a ukulele or run away from a falling chimney stack while wearing clogs will he really be able to compete in this particular field.

# THE NORTHERN CULTURE GUIDE

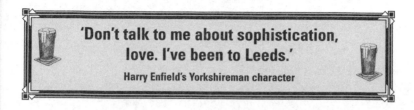

'Don't talk to me about sophistication, love. I've been to Leeds.'

Harry Enfield's Yorkshireman character

You know us northerners, right? We don't know much about art, but we know what we bloody well like. A spot of *Agadoo* on the karaoke, a rugby league match on a Saturday and a racist comedian down the working men's club. Nowt fancy, like, but it's grand for the likes of us.

Is it fuck.

The North has been producing talented writers, musicians and artists for hundreds of years, serving up an all-you-can-eat buffet of genius for southerners to gorge on.

The literary tradition of the North dates back to Bede's *Ecclesiastical History of the English People*, and the medieval poems *Pearl* and *Sir Gawain and the Green Knight*. The North has been home to movements such as the Romantics, like Wordsworth and Coleridge, who pondered the beauty of the Lake District, and the New Romantics, like The Human

League and ABC, who pondered the beauty of waitresses in cocktail bars.

In the mid nineteenth century, the Brontë sisters showed that there's more to romance in Yorkshire than getting a knee-trembler in a Ford Capri. And the region's literary excellence continued in the twentieth century with Ted Hughes, Tony Harrison and Simon Armitage proving that northern poetry doesn't end with 'stand up if you hate Chelsea' and 'who ate all the pies?'

And while southerners might assume that theatres in the North are used mainly to host pantomimes starring Cannon and Ball and some knobend from *Hollyoaks*, the North also has a respected theatre scene. Many major playwrights have come from up here, including Alan Bennett, Shelagh Delaney, Jim Cartwright, Willy Russell, John Godber and J. B. Priestley, and Alan Ayckbourn even had to move to Scarborough from London to start his career.

We've done our bit for British cinema too, with the brilliant but grim kitchen sink dramas of the sixties like *A Kind of Loving*, *A Taste of Honey* and *Saturday Night and Sunday Morning*. And if the formula of plucky northern underdog overcoming skepticism to triumph as a male stripper/ballet dancer/conductor of a colliery brass band has been a tad overdone recently, it's at least made for more entertaining viewing than the mockney gangster films that southerners churn out.

Much of Britain's finest acting talent also comes from round our way, including Dame Judy Dench, Jane Horrocks, David Thewlis and Sir Ian McKellen, who sadly failed to revert to his original Burnley accent when playing Gandalf in *Lord of the Rings*, so we missed him shouting, 'You shall not pass unless you want your head twatting in, you big bastard Balrog.'

And contrary to plain-speaking stereotypes, we *do* know much about art. That's why we've managed to produce painters like L. S. Lowry and David Hockney, sculptors like Henry Moore and people who sell pickled livestock for millions of pounds like Damien Hirst. It's also why a sculpture like the

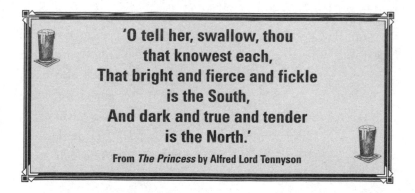

'O tell her, swallow, thou
that knowest each,
That bright and fierce and fickle
is the South,
And dark and true and tender
is the North.'

From *The Princess* by Alfred Lord Tennyson

*Angel of the North* can become so important to the kind of northern community that Brian Sewell thinks have no appreciation of art beyond that poster of the tennis bird scratching her arse from Athena.

There's more to northern music than the local pit's brass band, too. We've got opera companies like Opera North in Leeds, and Britain's oldest symphony orchestra, The Hallé, in Manchester. But if we're getting on to the topic of music, it's probably time to mention that the North has produced the greatest pop and rock the world has ever seen. The first Stone Roses album – now *that's* art . . .

**'Manchester's got everything except a beach.'**

Ian Brown, pop star

# Northern Rock:
# THE NORTHERN MUSIC GUIDE

**For over five decades the North has been producing the best music in the world. But for those who don't know their La's from their Elbow, or had forgotten that music was invented in the North, here's a whistle-stop tour of the cities and the bands that put our great region at the forefront of rock.**

Any tour of northern music must of course begin in **Liverpool** with The Beatles, a band that shaped a generation, symbolized an era, changed popular culture and made the word 'beetles' look as if was misspelled. The 'Pool's music scene has been brimming with psychedelic inventiveness ever since, with The Teardrop Explodes, Wah!, Echo and the Bunnymen, The La's, Shack, The Zutons and The Coral all unafraid to rock in the intimidating shadow of The Fabs. And none of them, with the exception of the drummer from Frankie Goes to Hollywood, looked like Scousers are supposed to.

Moving north-east, it's worth noting that in the seventies **Wigan** was the centre of the Northern Soul scene, which involved dancing all night to obscure American soul classics in the Casino nightclub. Although the scene is remembered as a northern music milestone, none of the artists it celebrated were locals, and were more likely to be singing about heartache and tainted love than eating a really satisfying meat and potato pie.

Moving east, we come to **Manchester**, a city that's been churning out great music as though bangin' tunes were a natural resource. Although they were southerners, The Sex Pistols can be credited with inspiring the city's famous music scene with their gig at The Lesser Free Trade Hall in 1976. While the gig itself was only attended by about forty people, it would have sold out Old Trafford many times over if you believe everyone who claims to have been there. From the punk and post-punk scenes that the show inspired came The Buzzcocks, Magazine, Joy Division, New Order, The Fall and Simply Red, the only one of these bands who stayed true to the punk agenda of creating music that would truly inspire hatred in the listener.

With the money made from Joy Division and New Order, Factory Records honchos Tony Wilson and Rob Gretton opened The Hacienda nightclub, where you could take Ecstasy and dance like a bellend to house music. This in turn inspired the 'Madchester' scene of bands such as The Happy Mondays and The Stone Roses, who created soaring, celebratory dance rock anthems. Although, given the amount of E the fans were taking, the beeping of a pelican crossing would probably have sounded soaring and celebratory.

A couple of years later came Oasis, a band so huge they even got soft southerners affecting the Manc accent and walking around like Gerry Anderson was controlling them. The Manchester indie scene continues with the beardy likes of Badly Drawn Boy, Doves and Elbow taking the baton.

Continuing east, we come to 'steel city' **Sheffield**, whose clanking industry inspired electronica from The Human League and Heaven 17 to Warp Records. The city is also notable for the sly, cynical humour in the lyrics of Pulp and The Arctic Monkeys and the unintentional comedy of Def Leppard, a band loved by people who use the word 'raunchy' without a hint of irony.

Your next pop-stop would have to be **Leeds**. As well as producing indie acts like The Wedding Present, Kaiser Chiefs and The Music, the city is renowned as the unholy centre of British goth music. Some claim that the goth scene took root in Yorkshire because it's where Dracula first came to the UK. Others claim that they're all a bunch of overweight virgins and the closest they come to evil in real life is refusing to turn their music down when their dad asks them.

Moving up to **Newcastle**, we find Brian Johnson from AC/DC, Neil Tennant from The Pet Shop Boys and Sting from before he started going on about having tantric sex in rainforests. Then you cross the border into Scotland and enter a musical wasteland of bagpipes, tin whistles and Runrig.

But stick within the boundaries of the North, and you'll find a huge range of great music from punk to baggy to hard rock. Nowhere else in the world has produced more great bands per square mile, and the only crap pop you'll find up here is Tesco Value cola.

### 'Everything is brilliant in Leeds.'
**Kaiser Chiefs T-shirt slogan**

# THE NORTH–SOUTH MUSIC DIVIDE

It's time to decide once and for all whether the North or the South is better at music with this completely fair and impartial comparison of musical highlights by decade.★

★Due to space restrictions, the following northern acts could not be included in the comparison: Simply Red, PJ and Duncan, Gareth Gates, Chris Waddle, Atomic Kitten, Robson Green, Rick Astley, Sonia, The Reynolds Girls, Mels B and C, Black Lace, Smokie, Ken Dodd, Cilla Black, Claire and Friends, Pete Waterman and St Winifred's School Choir.

'Oi! Vera Duckworth, put your clogs on and go feed t'whippets!'

**Donna Noble in *Doctor Who***

| DECADE | THE NORTH | THE SOUTH |
| --- | --- | --- |
| Sixties | The Beatles, Gerry and the Pacemakers, The Hollies, Herman's Hermits | Des O'Connor, Cliff Richard, Adam Faith, Pinky and Perky |
| Seventies | Joy Division, Magazine, The Buzzcocks, The Teardrop Explodes, Echo and the Bunnymen | David Essex, The Wombles, The Wurzels, Benny Hill, Clive Dunn |
| Eighties | The Smiths, The Happy Mondays, The Stone Roses, James, The La's, The Fall, The Human League, New Order, ABC | Chas and Dave, Anita Dobson, The Grange Hill Cast, Nick Berry |
| Nineties | Oasis, Badly Drawn Boy, Doves, Shack, Pulp, The Verve | Geri Halliwell, Mr Blobby, Bob the Builder, Dane Bowers, Victoria Beckham, Mr C from The Shamen, Martine McCutcheon, Emma Bunton |
| Noughties | The Zutons, The Coral, Arctic Monkeys, Elbow, Kaiser Chiefs | H from Steps, Vanilla, Steve Brookstein, Blue, The Fast Food Rockers |

# ONLY SOME NORTHERN SONGS

You can shove your Wonderwalls up your arse. These are the real anthems of the North. Not all of them would be welcome if they came up on shuffle. In fact, some might inspire you to throw your iPod on the floor and stamp on it to make sure that you never hear them again. But they're all songs about the North, and most of them are so northern they wouldn't seem out of place being played by a colliery brass band at a workers' picnic.

### 'Only a Northern Song' by The Beatles

Although many Beatles songs, from 'Penny Lane' to 'Strawberry Fields Forever', referenced places in the North, this George Harrison composition is the only one that concerned the entire region, with its apologetic lyrics about being a bit rubbish because it's only a northern song. It serves as a sarcastic attack on southerners who expect things from the North to be crap, as well as a veiled dig at Lennon and McCartney, whose publishing company was called Northern Songs.

### 'Fog on the Tyne' by Gazza and Lindisfarne

While many Geordies are understandably proud of their city's rich heritage, one aspect of it they certainly shouldn't be proud of is its hip hop heritage. Whether it's Ant and Dec's empty threats to wreck the mic or Gazza lisping his way through 'Fog on the Tyne', this is one group of east coast rappers who all deserve shooting. But no matter how awful this record was, Paul Gascoigne will always be fondly remembered for his performance in the 1990 World Cup, where he taught northern men the important lesson that it's okay to cry, but only about football.

## 'It's Grim up North' by The JAMs

This 1991 rave hit by The JAMs (aka The KLF) lists the names of towns and cities in the North before segueing into the hymn 'Jerusalem'. In the light of this upbeat climax and the caption 'The North will rise again' that concluded the video, most northerners understood the irony of the title. Southerners, on the other hand, thought, 'Yes, it is bladdy grim, isn't it? I've heard they don't even have any Chez Gérards.'

## 'Matchstalk Men and Matchstalk Cats and Dogs' by Brian and Michael

A song about L. S. Lowry, referencing Ancoats and Salford, sung by men in flat caps and featuring a brass band and St Winfred's School choir singing 'The Big Ship Sails', this single was so northern it was only audible to whippets and Fred Dibnah. Despite this, it managed to spend two weeks at number one back in the days when 'E' was just something that Mancunian musicians said at the start of sentences.

> ### 'In Liverpool, the difference between a funeral and a wedding is one less drunk.'
> **Paul O'Grady, comedian and TV host**

### 'Beer 'n' Sex 'n' Chips 'n' Gravy' by The Macc Lads

Still the only song ever to be written about the erotic power of covering fried potatoes in gravy. And who wouldn't be turned on by the sight of a big fat sweaty pie-eating bastard staggering around outside the chippie after closing time and spilling gravy down his jeans? Form a queue, girls.

### 'Scarborough Fair' by Simon and Garfunkel

Traditional northern ballad that has provided a hit for artists such as Simon and Garfunkel. The Scarborough Fair that the song refers to was a huge annual gathering of tradesmen from around the world that took place in the Middle Ages. It's got nothing to do with the funfair that currently stands in Scarborough, which is why the lyrics don't go 'Parsley, sage, rosemary and a group of teenagers drinking cider behind the Hook-a-Duck'.

### 'The Anfield Rap' by Liverpool FC

Rapping and football are two activities that require a tremendous amount of skill, and the chance of someone being able to do both well is incredibly slim.

The chance of an entire team being able to do both well is virtually nil and so it proved with Liverpool FC's 1988 single

'The Anfield Rap (Red Machine in Full Effect)'. The single reached number three on the charts, confirming the stereotype that Scousers like to wallow in disaster.

## 'Come on you Reds' by Manchester United and Status Quo

While Liverpool FC didn't quite have the skills to pay the bills, they at least tried harder than Man United in their 1994 single. In the video for this, the Reds look so static and awkward that the moment Lee Sharpe attempts a spot of air guitar is included twice. Maybe a better title would have been 'Come on you Reds (Put a Bit of Effort into this Novelty Single you've been Forced to Appear on)'. And it's strange that, given the wealth of great music from Manchester itself, United had to travel as far as Catford to find collaborators, although I'm sure they count as a local band to most fans.

## 'Dirty Old Town' by Ewan McColl

Although this song is associated with Ireland due to famous versions by The Pogues and The Dubliners, it was originally written about Salford by folk singer Ewan McColl in 1949. The song evokes the kind of grimy industrial town that now only exists in the misconceptions of southerners. Listening to it these days, you can only imagine that the factory's been converted into luxury studio flats with a security guard and a gym, the docks have been rebranded as 'quays' and if you wanted to dream a dream by the old canal there would be a handy branch of Costa for you to do it in.

### 'The Light at the End of the Tunnel (is the Light of an Oncoming Train)' by Half Man Half Biscuit

While the JAMs might have scored a novelty hit by listing obscure northern towns, Half Man Half Biscuit have made a career out of it. It's hard to pick a particular song, but this one deserves to make the list for mentioning Matlock Bath, Eyam, Leek and New Mills, slagging off people from Notting Hill *and* having the dourest song title ever. Now that, Lennon and McCartney, is a northern song.

'I really don't like the North of England. It's always raining, it's very cold and I don't like all those little houses.'
**Frédérica Kanouté, footballer**

# THE NORTHERN TELLY HALL OF FAME

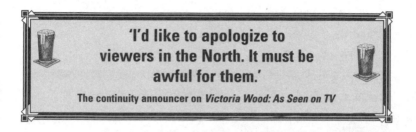

'I'd like to apologize to
viewers in the North. It must be
awful for them.'

The continuity announcer on *Victoria Wood: As Seen on TV*

In the early days of television, the only way to see
a northerner on the telly was to turn it off and
look at your reflection. But when the influence of
'kitchen sink' dramatists like John Osbourne
reached TV in the early sixties, you couldn't turn
on the box without seeing headscarves, pregnant
teens, tin baths and drunken fathers saying, 'Less o'
that bloody lip or I'll tek my belt to you.' Here are
a few northern telly landmarks.

## Brookside
The Scouse soap is now chiefly remembered for men with
bubble perms, moustaches and shell suits telling each other to
calm down, which is grossly unfair. Some of them actually wore
jeans and T-shirts.

## Coronation Street

Britain's most popular soap opera, despite what fans of moaning cockneys might claim. *Coronation Street* was created by Tony Warren in 1960 in an effort to bring gritty realism to serial drama. These days it's about as close to gritty realism as *Teletubbies*, but however silly it gets we'll always hold it close in our affections for giving us great northern icons like Elsie Tanner, Annie Walker, Vera Duckworth and Bet Lynch.

## Emmerdale

When it began in the early seventies, *Emmerdale Farm* as it was then known, was a gentle lunchtime soap in which a tractor getting stuck in mud was considered cliffhanger material. But when Phil Redmond took over as producer in 1993, he crashed a plane into the village and transformed the show into a ratings smash. Since then the village of Emmerdale has seen so many sieges, storms, kidnappings and murders that you'd have to wonder if it was built on an Indian burial ground.

## Z Cars

Devised as a response to the sedate *Dixon of Dock Green*, Merseyside's *Z Cars* is regarded as the first gritty police drama. It wasn't exactly *The Wire*, but it was an important step in the evolution of TV cops from reassuringly paternal bobbies who gave people directions to hard-drinking bastards who beat confessions out of people and pretend they fell downstairs.

## The Adventures of Sherlock Holmes

Although not regarded as a northern show, *The Adventures of Sherlock Holmes* was actually made in Manchester by Granada Television, as were other adaptations such as *Jeeves and Wooster*, *Jewel in the Crown* and *Brideshead Revisited*. Granada resisted the temptation to set these classics in the local area, so we never got to see Holmes and Moriarty's epic fight relocated from the Reichenbach Falls to the precinct outside Wetherspoons.

## Life on Mars

Hybrid of sci-fi and crime drama about Manc copper Sam Tyler getting hit by a car in 2006 and waking up in the year 1973. Tyler then had to survive as a police detective in a Manchester of hard drinking, chain smoking, sexism and racism. Viewers in the North wondered how he would possibly cope. Viewers in the South wondered how he would possibly tell the difference.

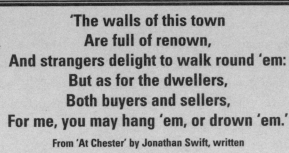

'The walls of this town
Are full of renown,
And strangers delight to walk round 'em:
But as for the dwellers,
Both buyers and sellers,
For me, you may hang 'em, or drown 'em.'

**From 'At Chester' by Jonathan Swift, written**

**over 250 years before *Hollyoaks***

## Hollyoaks

Soap set in a Chester suburb where a local genetic deformity has made all the girls look like *FHM* models and the blokes look like boyband members. It's not yet known what causes this tragic condition, but scientists believe they might be able to find an explanation and possible cure by comparing the Chester outbreak to similar cases in Summer Bay, Ramsay Street and on the Costa Eldorado.

## The League of Gentlemen

Classic sketch show set in Royston Vasey, whose freakish, inbred inhabitants engaged in murder, cannibalism, incest, wife kidnapping, urine drinking, community theatre and vampirism. In other words, it was the North's second most frightening village after Emmerdale.

## Byker Grove

Children's drama set in a youth club in the Byker area of Newcastle upon Tyne, which traumatized an entire generation when Ant McPartlin's character PJ was blinded in a paintball accident. They were traumatized again a few years later when they saw the videos to PJ and Duncan's singles 'Let's Get Ready to Rhumble', 'U Krazy Katz' and 'Eternal Love', which made them want to take a paintball gun to their own eyes.

## The Wheeltappers and Shunters Social Club

Let's not pretend that all northern telly deserves classic status. Produced by Granada in the mid-seventies, *The Wheeltappers and Shunters Social Club* is an example of the kind of show that made southerners believe we were all thick. Set in a fictional working men's club, each episode would feature sweaty racist comedians like Bernard Manning, washed-up fifties crooners and variety acts attempting to string out a single gimmick into an entire career. Alternative comedy might have become too preachy at times, but *The Wheeltappers and Shunters Social Club* shows why it had to happen.

# THE WILDLIFE OF THE NORTH

The North has produced many celebrated animal-lovers, from Sir Paul McCartney to Morrissey to the vets from *All Creatures Great and Small*. And it's not surprising, given the diversity of wildlife we've got up here. Here are some of the animals you'll find north of the border.

### Diddymen

Mention the word 'Diddy' to a child these days, and they'll think of a narcissistic East Coast rapper. But a few years back, they would have thought of the race of tiny creatures who toil in the jam butty mines of Knotty Ash that were discovered by comedian Ken Dodd.

The Diddymen fell on hard times after Thatcher closed the jam butty mines in the mid eighties. Recent attempts to re-employ them in call centres have stalled as their jocular high voices freak people out.

### Gromits

A variety of beagle found in the North that's born without a mouth and is forced to communicate through comic facial expressions. A Gromit was recently discovered who had been forced to drive, perform DIY and operate heavy machinery by its owner, a Mr Wallace, who has since been imprisoned.

## Pigeons

In kitchen-sink dramas, downtrodden fathers would often escape to their pigeon lofts when they grew tired of telling everyone that kids these days have gone soft. As with whippets, there is some truth behind the stereotype, as many northerners do indeed keep homing pigeons. And any bird that immediately returns to the North wherever you take it surely deserves a place in this hall of fame.

## Blue Meanies

Animated creatures that starred in The Beatles movie *Yellow Submarine*. In it, they launch a surprise attack on the undersea kingdom of Pepperland by enclosing it in a music-proof bubble. Recent attempts have been made to locate the Blue Meanies and ask them to enclose Sir Paul McCartney in a music-proof bubble so we don't have to hear any more of his solo albums, but sadly the species cannot currently be located.

## Whippets

Whippets are the breed of dog that's most associated with the North, and that's hardly surprising given that they're strong, healthy and never have thick coats. Many people up here still race whippets, so for once there's some truth in the stereotype. Although they don't wear clogs and flat caps while doing it, so it's not entirely accurate.

## Monkeys

Despite giving northerners their most famous nickname, there are relatively few actual monkeys in the region. The only primate from the North to have achieved any kind of fame so far has been Cuddles, a bright orange monkey who appeared on *The Keith Harris Show* and *Cuddles and Company* in the eighties. Cuddles suggests that there might be an entire colony of aggressive orange monkeys living somewhere in the wild and moaning about how they 'hate that duck', but no evidence of it has been found yet.

## Flumps

Small furry balls with arms and legs that featured on TV show *The Flumps*, which was screened in the seventies and eighties. These mysterious creatures engaged in stereotypical northern behaviour such as moaning about the weather, wearing flat caps and playing brass instruments. There have been no reported sightings of flumps since the eighties, and it's thought that the species might have died out as their slow movement and high centre of gravity made them an easy target for predators.

## LIVERPOOL SALAD

A recent slang trend has been to use the name of a local town that you consider to be especially downmarket to create a term for something pikey. This practice probably derives from the term 'Glasgow kiss', meaning head butt. The names of the towns in question will obviously vary depending on where the term is created, so the following are only intended as examples.

Doncaster picnic – eating fish and chips at a bus stop
Wakefield shower – spraying Lynx on instead of washing
Liverpool salad – chips
Middlesbrough toothbrush – chewing gum
Wigan limo – bus
Stockport briefcase – plastic bag
Sunderland steak – kebab

## Ferrets

Long, lean mammals that were once used extensively in the North for rabbit hunting. Thousands remain in the region today, most of which are kept as pets. Although I'm sure some southerners believe that we're so poor we still have to send them down rabbit holes to fetch us a myxomatosis-ridden snack.

## Kestrels

As anyone who's ever seen a film about the North knows, most of us train kestrels in an effort to transcend our humdrum lives. But then our older brothers kill them, and we have to take up ballet dancing instead.

## Yorkshire Terriers

It's a constant source of shame for tough Yorkshiremen that their proud county gives its name to this breed of small dog. The German town of Rottweil gets the hardest dog on the estate named after it, and what does Britain's largest county get? Those yappy little bastards that old ladies have.

# THE NORTHERN MONKEY STYLE GUIDE

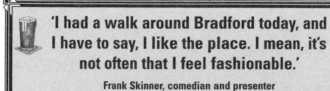

'I had a walk around Bradford today, and I have to say, I like the place. I mean, it's not often that I feel fashionable.'

**Frank Skinner, comedian and presenter**

One of the areas of northern life that southerners have the greatest misconceptions about is fashion. Some ignorant Southern Jessies still think that the North is full of men wearing flat caps, clogs, string vests and trousers (held up by braces) with enough room to shove a couple of ferrets down. And even those who understand we've surged out of the nineteenth century tend to imagine that style in the top half of the country means stonewashed denim, earrings in the shape of Nike swooshes, and gold chains so fake that they leave a green stain around your neck. Take, for example, the following joke, guaranteed to fetch a braying, superior laugh from a southerner: 'What do you call a Scouse woman in a white shell suit? The bride.'

The truth is that the North is much more style-conscious than London's fashionistas think. Northern designers such as Wayne Hemingway and Vivienne Westwood have shown poncey southern designers a thing or two. And let's not forget that we gave the world fashions such as the moptop haircuts of the Merseybeat scene, the bowling shirts and brogues of the Northern Soul scene and the baggy clothing of the Madchester scene, which was so bright and psychedelic it was often difficult to tell if you'd taken any drugs or not when you saw a nightclub full of it.

The sartorial sophistication of the North was highlighted in 1996, when Leeds was chosen as the location of the first Harvey Nichols store outside of London, and it became such a status symbol that many locals would hang on to the bags from there and use them for their TK Maxx and Primark shopping.

However, there is one preconception about northern style that's pretty hard to deny. No matter how freezing it is, we don't put a lot of layers on. Walk around a town centre in the North on any Saturday night and you'll see groups of lads in T-shirts and girls in skimpy dresses regardless of weather conditions. This could be because as soon as they get inside their local meat market nightclub, they're hit with the combined body heat given off two hundred people doing 'big fish, little fish, cardboard box' to bad techno. It could be that northerners are worried that if they wear their coats now they won't feel the benefit later, in the next ice age. Or it could simply be because northerners are harder than southerners, and less likely to reach for their parkas at the first sign of light drizzle. This is especially apparent when a northern football team plays a southern team in winter and you see rows of southern fans shivering in arctic clothing facing rows of northern fans who've found the conditions so sweltering that they've chosen to take their football shirts off and swing them around their heads.

But perhaps the most likely reason that northerners don't like wearing coats is because they don't want to cover up their fancy outfits. In the North, getting dolled up for a night out is much more important. Especially on weekdays, where northerners will typically go home after work, eat their tea, get ready and meet up later on, while southerners are more likely to go straight to the pub in their dishevelled work clothes, pausing briefly to spray themselves with deodorant or daub lipstick on so quickly they look like Robert Smith. In the North, making an effort for a night out is a well-observed ritual.

Yes, sometimes the men dab on a bit too much aftershave and put on more gold chains than Jimmy Savile and P. Diddy combined. And yes, sometimes the women go so overboard with the fake tan that even David Dickinson would be bobby-dazzled. But at least they're doing it for the right reasons. To go out looking glammed up and ready for ten pints, a curry and a fight: a proper northern night.

## NORTHERN STYLE THROUGHOUT THE YEAR

| MONTH | TYPICAL DRESS |
|---|---|
| January | T-shirt and jeans/flimsy dress |
| February | T-shirt and jeans/flimsy dress |
| March | T-shirt and jeans/flimsy dress |
| April | T-shirt and jeans/flimsy dress |
| May | T-shirt and jeans/flimsy dress |
| June | T-shirt and jeans/flimsy dress |
| July | Pair of shorts/really flimsy dress |
| August | T-shirt and jeans/flimsy dress |
| September | T-shirt and jeans/flimsy dress |
| October | T-shirt and jeans/flimsy dress |
| November | T-shirt and jeans/flimsy dress |
| December | T-shirt, jeans and Santa hat/flimsy dress and Santa hat |

# NORTHERN STYLE CLASSICS

Here are a few items of clothing that will forever be associated with the North. I'm not suggesting that you should rush out and buy them now, but in their day, they were all fashion essentials.

### Flat caps

These infamous items of headgear are the unofficial emblem of the North. Like Burberry clothing, they were originally worn by country squires but became so widespread among the lower classes that they eventually came to signify poverty. Interestingly, they've been out of popular fashion so long that toffs have now started to wear them again. Perhaps they'll put the Burberry tartan back on soon.

### The 'football casual' look

The European success of Liverpool FC in the late seventies and early eighties lead to many fans bringing exotic sportswear back from their travels. Soon the terraces were filling up with clothing by Sergio Tacchini, Fila, Diadora and Lacoste, often in soothing pastel colours. The look caught on throughout the North, and before long the toughest kids in every town were dressing like Alan Partridge. By the mid eighties it became impossible to tell if someone was about to mug you or invite you to a pro-celebrity golf tournament.

## Clogs

Cheap items of wooden footwear that were popular during the Industrial Revolution. In the misconceptions of southerners, we still drag these across the rain-sodden cobbled streets, as we tuck into a slimy handful of tripe and make our way down to the mill.

## The Fred Perry polo shirt

A staple of the 'Northern soul' and 'football casual' looks, this shirt is one of the region's few fashion classics that was created in honour of a local. Next time you're deciding if a laurel or shark logo would look better on your moob, consider whether you'd rather celebrate the efforts of a man from Stockport who won eight Grand Slam singles titles, or a poncey French player called René Lacoste who only won seven.

## Joe Bloggs flares

It's ironic that Manchester, the city that gave the world cotton in the eighteenth century, was giving the world its most ludicrous waste of the stuff by the end of the twentieth century. Cashing in on the 'Madchester' scene of the late eighties, clothing company Joe Bloggs sold baggy sky-blue flared jeans by the truckload. They might have seemed cool when you bought them in Afflecks Palace, but after you'd spent a night dragging them through puddles and past overflowing urinals, their practical limitations became all too apparent.

## Kangol hats

Although the Kangaroo logo has led some to assume that Kangol is an Australian brand, the company was actually founded in Cleator, Cumbria. So it's apt that their 'bucket hat' became an icon of both Madchester, through the patronage of Stone Roses drummer Reni, and Britpop, through the patronage of Liam Gallagher. For a moment during the mid nineties, even the coolest fashionistas were wearing Kangol hats, flicking V-signs and calling everyone 'our kid' in a nasal voice.

## Shell suits

Elasticated nylon sports suits that were popular in the late eighties. Worn by hard northern estate kids, these items let everyone know you weren't afraid to be a fire hazard. A shell-suit wearer might rob you, or they might be exposed to a naked flame and turn into a human fireball. Either way you were in danger.

## Massive logos

Moving on to modern scally chic, it's difficult to single out a particular item. But one principle holds firm – you must be covered from head to toe in massive logos. From your baseball cap to your trainers, everything must display a clothing brand logo, and the logo must be as big as the bootlegger's screen-printing machine can make it.

Check your appearance before you leave the flat. If you look like a hoarding outside sportswear wholesalers, you've mastered scally chic.

### Trackie pants rolled into sports socks

Nothing will get people rushing out of their doors to tell you to get away from their cars faster than tucking your tracksuit bottoms into your sports socks. Nobody is quite sure why this became such a scally staple. Some believe that it allows them to shoplift more easily by shoving things down their tracksuit bottoms, but it's more likely that it simply gives them an opportunity to display yet another logo (see above).

### Moustaches

The North is one of the few places outside the Middle East where heterosexual men still sport moustaches. Perhaps they originally grew them in emulation of football heroes like Ian Rush, Mark Lawrenson and David Seaman. Perhaps they thought they would make them look like as masculine as Burt

Reynolds or Tom Selleck. Whatever the reason, we should all be proud to live in a region where men are comfortable enough with their sexuality to sport such camp facial furniture.

### ONCE UPON A TIME IN THE NORTH

A 2008 ITV survey found that the North is the nation's favourite fictional backdrop. Hardly surprising when you consider we've got Catherine Cookson country in South Tyneside, Brontë country in the West Yorkshire Pennines and *Crimewatch* country to the east of the Mersey Estuary.

# THE NORTHERN MONKEY HALL OF FAME:
# CELEBRITIES

Just a few decades ago, appearing on television with a regional accent was a social faux pas on the same scale as wearing an inappropriately bright hat to church, or murder. Things have changed a lot since then, and these days northerners are even allowed to appear on the news, although we're more likely to do the comedy final item about a waterskiing squirrel than read the headlines. Here are a few northerners who have been allowed on the telly.

### Christopher Eccleston

When *Doctor Who* finally overcame his deadliest foe (the BBC commissioning editor for drama) and returned to our screens in 2005, it was time for a proper northerner to step into the Tardis. The timelord's accent was even questioned by assistant Rose Tyler who asked him why he sounds like he's from the North if he's an alien, to which Eccleston replied, 'Lots of planets have a North.' Sadly this intriguing idea hasn't been explored on the show, and we're yet to see Daleks struggling around the cobbled streets of Northern Skaro or Cybermen from the North of Telos zapping each other for looking at their cybergirlfriends in the spaceship park at closing time.

## Derek Acorah

Scouse medium who hosts shows *Most Haunted* and *Ghost Towns*. Acorah has astonished TV viewers for years with his uncanny and completely inexplicable ability to channel the spirits of the dead. As long as the dead in question sound exactly like camp and sinister middle-aged men from the Merseyside area.

## Ant and Dec

The popular northern hosts started out in *Byker Grove* before launching themselves upon the hip hop world in 1994 with 'Let's Get Ready to Rhumble' in which they claimed they had so many lyrics they were 'frightened to use them'. At the time it seemed inconceivable that the duo would even be forgiven by their own parents for this atrocity. But to their credit, they eventually established themselves as the most popular light entertainers for a generation. Even if most of us won't get round to learning which one is which until one of them dies.

If you're struggling to remember which is which, I've devised a handy mnemonic that might help: Ant has a bulbous forehead like an ant, while Dec is small, like a decimal point.

## Kerry Katona

A *Jeremy Kyle* guest who seems to have mistakenly wandered into the arena of national celebrity, Katona holds a particular fascination for southerners, who love to sneer at a northern girl confirming all the hard-living pram-faced stereotypes. She was even voted Mum of the Year on two separate occasions, by people who wish their own mothers were a bit more like Shaun Ryder in a wig.

## Jimmy Savile

Leeds DJ who hosted *Top of the Pops* and *Jim'll Fix It*. At the time, many viewers were confused by his eccentric appearance and presenting style, but when the gangsta rap movement took off in the nineties, everyone took to wearing tracksuits and jewellery and muttering incoherently, and it turned out that Sir Jimmy was simply ahead of his time.

## Mick Hucknall

Thanks to the region's Viking ancestry, the North has a large ginger population, and many of them, including Stan Laurel, Rick Astley, Chris Evans and actual Northern Monkey Cuddles from *The Keith Harris Show*, have managed successful showbiz careers. But the most notorious northern copper-top is surely Simply Red singer Mick Hucknall, who didn't let his Manchester accent, hair colour or resemblance to Charlie Drake stop him from dating lots of posh women, and remains an inspiration to all unattractive northern men.

## The Chuckle Brothers

When Rotherham brothers Barry and Paul Elliot became the Chuckle Brothers, they created an act that would keep them in work for over three decades, but also make it very difficult for them to break out into serious dramatic roles. To this day, we've never seen Paul Chuckle in a moving and challenging reimagining of Ibsen or Barry Chuckle holding an RSC audience transfixed with the soliloquy, 'To you to me or not to you to me?'

## Morecambe and Wise

Northern double act who are always cited when people are moaning about how things like comedy, Christmas and the BBC aren't as good as they used to be. Their shows remain incredibly popular to this day with those who feel nostalgic for a more innocent time when two men could share a bed and enjoy a choreographed breakfast together without anyone assuming they were anything but close friends.

## Daniel Craig

Although he was born in Chester and grew up on the Wirral, Craig moved down to London to join the National Youth Theatre when he was a teenager and lost his Scouse accent. Which is a shame, because it's about time we saw James Bond kill a henchman and quip, 'Dey do die, dough, don't dey, dough?'

# TEN
# MISCONCEPTIONS
# ABOUT THE NORTH

As most southerners haven't actually bothered visiting the North, they imagine it to be populated by men returning home from t'pit with their faces covered in soot to women with rollers in their hair and wrinkly stockings scrubbing the front steps. This level of ignorance lets them believe a series of improbable myths about the North that place it somewhere in the late nineteenth century. If you're ever confronted with them, the best thing to do is just to let southerners believe them. That way, they're less likely to move up here and spoil it for the rest of us.

## Misconception #1: All shops in the North look like Arkwright's grocery from *Open All Hours*

The fact of the matter is that, for better or worse, all high streets in the UK look pretty much the same now. They've all got a Smith's, a Marks & Sparks and an independent fried chicken shop named after a random US state. Admittedly, Bond Street does still contain a few boutiques that you won't find in Barnsley, but those of us who buy our undies from Primark and our bacon from Tesco will be able to find most of what we're looking for in either the North or the South.

## Misconception #2: We still use outdoor toilets

The only time you'll see a northerner use an outdoor toilet is at Glastonbury, and even that isn't very likely as most of us are tough enough to hold it in for three days. Even if we've had twenty pints of pear cider, a tray of extra spicy veggie noodles and a bag of laxatives that are being marketed as 'legal highs'.

## Misconception #3: We don't have gas or electricity

Indoor toilets aren't the only things that southerners think we haven't got. While a southerner will hopefully be attempting a joke if they ask if we still use gas lighting, you could be asked in all seriousness if we've got HD telly, broadband or chains like Subway, Starbucks and Nando's yet. The best way to respond to this kind of ignorance is to look at them in mock amazement and then ask if it's true that in the South they have magical picture boxes in their living rooms and huge metal birds in the skies.

## Misconception #4: We're all bitter about the South being richer

Unless we happen to be watching *EastEnders*, most northerners are unlikely to waste much time worrying about what's going on in London. In fact, any southerners who've met northerners who appeared to have a chip on their shoulder about the South were probably boasting about how rich they are at the time.

## Misconception #5: We ate all the pies

You get a pretty grim impression of northern diet from the media. In 2006, *The Sun* printed pictures of mums in Rawmarsh near Rotherham pushing junk food through school railings after chips and pies were banned as part of Jamie Oliver's healthy eating campaign. Add to this the sight of Kerry Katona eyeing up trays of Chicken Dippers as though they were made of gold in Iceland ads and you'd think we were all hooked on the kind of diet that will have you in the ground before you're fifty. In fact, cuisine in the North has become significantly more sophisticated in the last few years, with posh supermarket chains like Waitrose expanding, several restaurants being awarded Michelin stars and Greggs introducing a low-fat range of sausage rolls.

## Misconception #6: We're not PC

In the minds of smug southerners, most northern men expect their wives to have their tea on the table when they get back from work, don't eat foreign muck and would call you a poof if you wore anything more outré than a shell suit. And while any region that's produced both Bernard Manning and Roy 'Chubby' Brown can't be entirely free of bigotry, you'll find that most of us are pretty tolerant these days.

Any southerners who doubt the PC credentials of the North should be forced to spend time in the West Yorkshire market town of Hebden Bridge, Britain's most right-on town. Instead of the clogs and whippets they might expect, they'll find environmental sustainability seminars, aromatherapy centres and awareness–raising groups. If anyone up there ever invites you to a 'workshop' don't bring your toolbox. You'll probably end up wearing a leotard and learning the Alexander Technique.

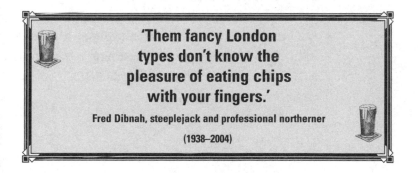

'Them fancy London types don't know the pleasure of eating chips with your fingers.'

Fred Dibnah, steeplejack and professional northerner

(1938–2004)

## Misconception #7: We're dour

A rather confusing stereotype of northerners is that we're stern, serious and a bit miserable. And while we did indeed give the world Morrissey and Ian Curtis and inspire the poetry of Philip Larkin, the average northerner does very little to justify the stereotype. After all, we're the ones who smile and say hello to strangers. They're the ones who block out their fields of vision with broadsheets in case anyone tries to speak to them. Which of these sounds like the miserable bastards to you?

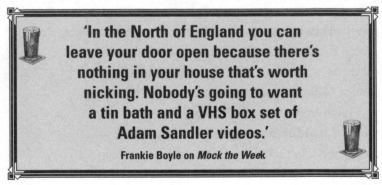

'In the North of England you can leave your door open because there's nothing in your house that's worth nicking. Nobody's going to want a tin bath and a VHS box set of Adam Sandler videos.'

Frankie Boyle on *Mock the Week*

## Misconception #8: We like to stick ferrets down t'pants

While many men have no doubt stuck ferrets down their trousers for a dare or for unpleasant personal reasons over the years, the notion that 'ferret legging' was ever a widespread sport in the North is a myth. However much you might want to believe urban legends, we're far less likely to stick furry animals down our pants than, say, Richard Gere.

## Misconception #9: We're covered in muck

In the perceptions of ignorant southerners, the North is still full of factories billowing out smog while men come back from t'pit with their faces blackened with soot that won't be removed until next Sunday's bath. This charge that the North is polluted is especially hard to take from Londoners, a group of people who were identified in a 2007 lecture by Dr Jim Smith from the Centre for Ecology and Hydrology as being more likely to suffer ill health from air pollution than the workers who were sent to clean up after the Chernobyl nuclear disaster.

The notion that the poisonous air that lot inhale is somehow cleaner than the fresh stuff we get up here takes the chuffing-well biscuit, but let them go on thinking it if they want. As long as they don't bring their Chelsea tractors up here and choke us to death too they can think what they want.

## Misconception #10: It always rains in the North

Whenever the North is shown in a film or on TV, it's always pissing it down, so it's not surprising that southerners think they'd need a brolly if they visited. But the statistics don't back this up. For example, although Manchester is known as 'the rainy city', its annual rainfall tends to be between 800 mm and 900 mm, much less than some southern cities like Plymouth, and even cities further afield like New York and Sydney. Anyway, the North must get plenty of sunshine – just look at the tans on David Dickinson, Peter Stringfellow and Julie Goodyear . . .

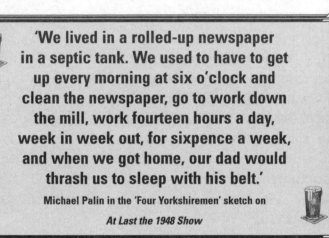

'We lived in a rolled-up newspaper in a septic tank. We used to have to get up every morning at six o'clock and clean the newspaper, go to work down the mill, work fourteen hours a day, week in week out, for sixpence a week, and when we got home, our dad would thrash us to sleep with his belt.'

Michael Palin in the 'Four Yorkshiremen' sketch on

*At Last the 1948 Show*

# THE FOOTBALL/ RELIGION GUIDE

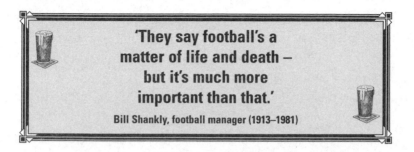

'They say football's a matter of life and death – but it's much more important than that.'

**Bill Shankly, football manager (1913–1981)**

It shouldn't come as much of a surprise that this famous quote comes from a one-time Liverpool FC manager. But even this hyperbole can't express how important football is in the North. In fact the only way you can really understand it is to listen to the roar a crowd of shirtless northern supporters makes when their team score. And then compare it with the polite smattering of applause the southern team they're playing get when they pull one back.

It's no surprise we care about football more. After all, we started it. Sheffield FC is officially recognized by FIFA as the world's oldest football club. Formed by members of Sheffield Cricket Club, they held their inaugural meeting on 24 October 1858 in Highfield. And 25 October 1858 was the first day that a fan complained that football isn't as good as it used to be, as foreign investment is taking the soul out of the game and players go down too easily these days.

And since then we've been consistently better at it. The North has still won the Premiership and the European Cup more than the South. Of course, this isn't a fact you hear being related much, because to do so would be to imply that you're proud of Manchester United in some way. And most northerners would sooner feel proud of Harold Shipman than Alex Ferguson.

While their fans understandably worship them, United are pretty much despised by everyone else in the North, who mutter bitterly whenever they chase another treble, quadruple, quintuple or sextuple, and tell jokes like this:

*Which three English football teams have swear words in their names?*
Arsenal, Scunthorpe and Manchester Fucking United.

Down South, however, most people love them, and some pubs even show United matches on their screens in favour of local teams. This is understandable in places like the West Country, but it seems strange if you come from London and could do your

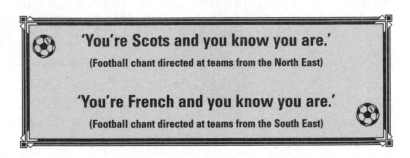

**'You're Scots and you know you are.'**
(Football chant directed at teams from the North East)

**'You're French and you know you are.'**
(Football chant directed at teams from the South East)

glory-hunting closer to home. Plus, it just doesn't quite sound right to overhear someone saying, 'Oh facking hell, Tarquin, I can't believe the referee gave City that penalty.'

The success of northern teams attracts some of the world's best players and managers to the region, leading to some bizarre hybrid accents combining Italian and Geordie, or Spanish and Scouse. This phenomenon can also happen in reverse, as when York native Steve McClaren moved to Holland to manage FC Twente and was soon talking with a spectacularly annoying Dutch-Yorkshire accent. Although he might just have been putting a silly voice on to avoid being recognized as Steve McClaren.

So, given that we invented football and we're better at it, why should the national stadium be all the way down in Wembley? If the stadium was up here, we'd have managed to get it finished quicker, and the matches would have a better atmosphere, with proper fans cheering the team on rather than leaving their seats empty after twenty minutes as they swan off for more champagne and prawn sandwiches in the corporate hospitality area.

Surely it would be much fairer to put the national stadium where the first football club was formed: Sheffield. That way, when southerners bang on about how football's coming home, they'd actually be telling the truth.

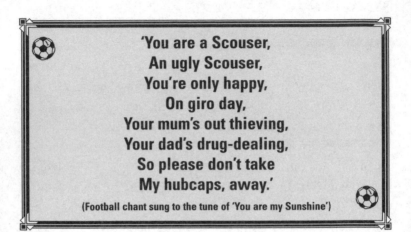

'You are a Scouser,
An ugly Scouser,
You're only happy,
On giro day,
Your mum's out thieving,
Your dad's drug-dealing,
So please don't take
My hubcaps, away.'
(Football chant sung to the tune of 'You are my Sunshine')

# I Predict a Diet:
# The Northern Cuisine Guide

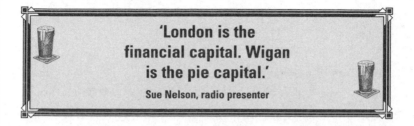

> 'London is the
> financial capital. Wigan
> is the pie capital.'
>
> **Sue Nelson, radio presenter**

**Despite what you might have heard, there's more to northern cuisine than tripe, pigs' trotters and dripping.**

Like the rest of the UK, northerners have acquired a taste for more upmarket food in the past couple of decades, and these days we're just as likely to buy sun-blushed tomatoes and organic houmous from Marks & Spencer Simply Food as take our chances with some unmarked tins from Lidl. Some restaurants even put tables and chairs outside on the pavements now, so we can all feel like we're dining out in Paris. Although the Champs Elysées has slightly fewer old people on mobility scooters complaining that you're in their way.

Not that traditional northern cuisine is anything to be ashamed of, mind. The North is home to several dishes that southerners wouldn't touch unless you made up a French name for them. Like Lancashire hot pot, a slow-baked blend of meat, carrots, potatoes and onions that most southerners assume was invented by the writers of *Coronation Street* in much the same way that lembas bread was invented by Tolkien. Or lobscouse, the aforementioned meat stew that gave Scousers their name. Or black pudding, a mixture of onions, pork fat, oatmeal and congealed pig's blood that was used as a weapon in the northern martial art of Ecky Thump in *The Goodies*.

Even if a sophisticated palate might find these dishes bland, they're surely preferable to the kind of traditional fayre served down South, like cockles, mussels and jellied eels. These foods could only ever have gained popularity in a city of masochists who travel to work every morning with their faces in each other's armpits and make folk heroes of the gangsters who kneecap them.

And it's not just local specialities that make the cuisine of the North different. While chips are available throughout the UK, proper chips are only available in the North. That's because they're made by chopping potatoes up rather than pouring a large bag of polystyrene shavings into the deep fat fryer. And, yes, for what it's worth, we do strange things to them like cover them in gravy, cut them into round shapes and call them 'scallops' and stick them between a couple of slices of bread to create the chip butty, an item of food that you're not even allowed to see if you're on the Atkins diet. All this interest in fried food might not sound very healthy, and to be honest it's not, but when it comes to these matters we prefer to compare ourselves to the Scots, who regard something as health food if it's only been battered and deep-fried once.

So if you're planning a visit, southerners, there's no need to pack emergency rations of fennel and ciabatta. It's highly likely that you'll be able to find the food you're looking for up here. Unless you're looking for jellied eels, in which case you're a dirty cockney bastard who doesn't deserve to be fed at all.

'I enjoyed the subtle delicacies that are the carefully chosen delicacy of them as would become perfect in body and mind – black pudding, chip butties, tripe and a piece of parkin for afters.'

From *The Goodies* episode 'Kung Fu Capers', about the northern martial art Ecky Thump

# TEN NORTHERN DELICACIES YOU MUST TRY

Don't knock the traditional delicacies of the North until you've tried them. Try them and then knock them.

### Chip Butty

Recent healthy-eating fads have all but killed off the traditional chip butty. Perhaps if we made them with brown bread, low-fat margarine and a salad garnish, we might be allowed to eat them again. Or perhaps we should just say, 'Fuck it, I could go under a bus tomorrow, I'm having a chip butty, a lard pasty and a side order of lard.'

### Vimto

You can forget your Coke and Pepsi, the North has a soft drink of its own in Vimto. Originally marketed as medicine called Vim Tonic in 1908, Vimto caught on as a fizzy drink instead, and we've been glugging it down with our chips and gravy ever since. Admittedly, it might not be as healthy as the cranberry and pomegranate smoothies southerners drink, and its name is an anagram of 'vomit', but it's ours, and we'll continue to drink it out of loyalty.

## Kendal Mint Cake

Available in gift shops throughout the Lake District, the taste of Kendal Mint Cake instantly conjures up misty fells, dark meres and men with beards telling you that you're wearing the wrong kind of shoes to go walking in.

## Pigs' trotters

In poorer times, it was accepted that no part of an animal should go to waste, and recipes were devised for consuming them from 'nose to tail'. In the case of pigs, this meant that their cheeks, intestines, tails and trotters became popular dishes. These days most young northerners wouldn't entertain the notion of putting such things in their mouths, although they'll be happy to eat much worse parts of animals if you call them things like 'nuggets' or 'twizzlers'.

## Tripe

What could be more appetizing than the lining from the first three chambers of a cow's stomach? You can fry tripe, boil it with onions, put it in soup, or try not to think about it ever again in case you vom down your shirt.

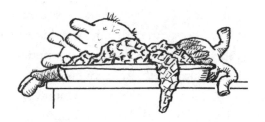

## The Steak Bake from Greggs

Founded in the 1930s in Newcastle, Greggs has now expanded into a chain of over a thousand shops, and there are even a couple of branches in Belgium. Some people are now predicting that Greggs will become the North's own Starbucks, and spark a wave of northern cultural imperialism that will see cool kids all over the world tucking into cheese and onion pasties at bus stops while wearing Umbro tracksuits.

## Black pudding

Eating a sausage made out of congealed blood might not sound very appetizing, but try telling that to the people of Bury in Lancashire, who eat it for breakfast, lunch and tea. Some have even speculated that Bury could be the place that *The League of Gentlemen* butcher Hilary Briss relocated after he fled Royston Vasey in 2000 and that Bury black pudding is in fact his infamous 'special stuff'. No sightings of Briss have been confirmed, but local police are ready to swoop if a nosebleed epidemic breaks out.

## Yorkshire pudding

Originally cooked underneath a large joint to catch dripping fat, the Yorkshire pudding is as much a part of the great British Sunday as washing the car and watching pensioners slide down hillsides in baths. As with black pudding, white pudding and steak pudding, this is a savoury dish in spite of its name, so don't go ordering them as an alternative to your fennel natas, vanilla truffles and lychee baklavas, southerners.

## Bread and dripping

A traditional snack made out of the thick fat left over from cooking beef and pork, which is also known as a 'mucky sandwich' in Yorkshire. I'm sure the idea of consuming this type of thing will disgust southerners as they dip their rosemary and garlic focaccia into a bowl of organic olive oil in a fancy restaurant.

## Bitter

It's an unfortunate coincidence for northerners that the name of our favourite drink is also the name of the mindset southerners attribute to us. Still, we wouldn't mind asking for a pint of 'envious, brooding and impoverished' if it got us some lovely Tetley's, John Smith's or Boddies.

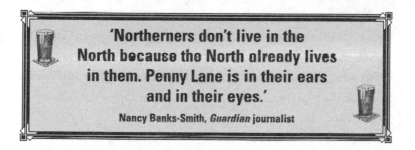

'Northerners don't live in the North because the North already lives in them. Penny Lane is in their ears and in their eyes.'

**Nancy Banks-Smith, *Guardian* journalist**

# THE NORTHERN MONKEY HALL OF FAME:
# HONORARY NORTHERNERS

**They didn't really come from the North, but we're prepared to bend the truth a little and pretend that they did, either because they came from very near the North, or because they influenced its culture.**

### Eric Cantona

Most northerners would sooner elevate Michael Winner to hero status than a Frenchman, but there's not much argument if he helps your club to win four premiership titles in five years. Although Cantona initially moved to Leeds from Auxerre, it's his stint with Manchester United for which he's still revered. Although some were initially worried about how he might adapt to the culture of Manchester, he soon blended in perfectly by mumbling incoherently about seagulls and lashing out violently at strangers.

### R. Kelly

The Chicago-based R'n'B star might not sound like a northerner, but he should be made an honorary one on account of his name. He's caused much confusion in northern households since his rise to fame, along the lines of 'What do you mean our Kelly was on MTV last night?' and 'What do you mean our Kelly pioneered the unintentionally hilarious hip-hopera genre?'

## Shakespeare

It's sometimes claimed that Shakespeare was a northerner, but this is stretching the geographical truth a bit. He was born in Stratford-upon-Avon, so he was surely a midlander rather than a northerner or southerner, and attempts to claim him for the North betray double standards. We're happy to include the Midlands in the North when we want to take credit for things like *King Lear*, heavy metal and baltis, but we're all too keen to distance ourselves from their more unfortunate points, like having the only British accent which makes you sound thick but not hard.

## J. R. R. Tolkien

As with Shakespeare, many would like to grant a special extension of the borders of the North to include the creator of modern fantasy, who was originally from Birmingham. Interestingly, when his books are adapted into films, the actors tend to put on West Country accents, whereas if they were going to stay true to Tolkien's origins, they should have cast Howard from the Halifax ads as Frodo, Benny from *Crossroads* as Sam, Jasper Carrot as Gollum and Ozzie Osbourne as Sauron.

## Craig David

The lukewarm R'n'B singer hails from Southampton, but his *Bo Selecta* caricature from Morley in Leeds became so well known at one point that it eclipsed the fame of the real Craig David. Some people assume Mel B from The Spice Girls was the victim of a similarly inaccurate northern caricature on the show, until they see her being interviewed and realize that she's actually like that.

## Philip Larkin

Although he was born in Coventry, the glum poet spent the last thirty years of his life in Hull, where he was the university librarian. The fishy city seems to be proud of the association, although Larkin was less so, once commenting, 'I wish I could think of just one nice thing I could tell you about Hull. Oh yes . . . it's very nice and flat for cycling.' Given the bleakness of his work, however, it's likely that Hull's grim reputation was the very thing that attracted Larkin in the first place. He probably just chose the place that could give him the maximum level of boredom to moan about in his poems.

## Samuel Taylor Coleridge

Although often classed as one of the Lake Poets, Coleridge originally hailed from Devonshire. Believing that art should take inspiration from nature, Coleridge moved to Keswick in the

Lake District. In doing so, he set a pattern of moving up North for a more creative life that retired city workers still follow today. The difference was that he took opium and produced works of hallucinatory genius, rather than eating houmous and painting shit watercolours.

## Boudica

Boudica, or Boadicea as we used to call her, was the queen of the Iceni tribe in East Anglia, so it's a bit of a stretch to claim her as a northerner. But she did lead a revolt against the occupying forces of the Roman Empire in AD 60 that culminated in her burning the whole of London to the ground. And if anyone deserves to be named as an honorary northerner, it's the woman who once destroyed London.

## Friedrich Engels

Beardy lefties in the North are especially proud of the region's associations with the co-founder of Communism. Engels moved to Manchester in 1842, and his experience of the city during the Industrial Revolution formed the basis of his book *The Condition of the Working Class of England in 1844*, and influenced *The Communist Manifesto*. But despite inspiring Communism, Mancs themselves never quite managed to have a revolution. Although they did get a bit narked when some Americans bought United.

## Anthony Gormley

Although sculptor Anthony Gormley was born in Kent, he went to school in Yorkshire, and many of his most famous works are located in the North. Like 'Another Place', a collection of a hundred cast-iron men staring out to the Irish Sea on Crosby Beach near Liverpool, and the *Angel of the North*, a huge steel sculpture in Gateshead. Although it caused some controversy when it was initially constructed, the *Angel of the North* has now been accepted as a major landmark of the North East and is regarded as the most extraordinary work of northern sculpture since Pete Burns's face.

# TURNED OUT SHITE AGAIN:
# THE NORTHERN WEATHER GUIDE

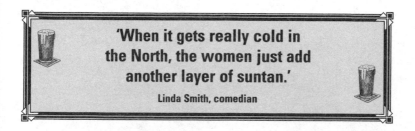

'When it gets really cold in the North, the women just add another layer of suntan.'

**Linda Smith, comedian**

When I first went to London I couldn't believe the difference in temperature. I had to mop the sweat from my brow, take my jacket off and tie it around my waist and create a fan out of a copy of the *Evening Standard* while my body adapted to the sweltering conditions. Then I got off the tube and I realized that the weather in the South was in fact exactly the fucking same. Not that you'd know from the way southerners go on.

It's about four hundred miles from the most northerly point of England to the most southerly point. This is admittedly quite a substantial distance, and anyone who walks it for charity certainly deserves their sponsorship money, but it's nothing compared to, say, the distance from New York to LA. From the way they talk about it you'd think that the country stretched all the way from Greenland to the Costa Del Sol, allowing them all to lounge by the pool all day while we have to hunt and skin polar bears to survive.

Perhaps this mass delusion about the climate explains the panic that grips the South if they do suffer a spot of bad weather. All it takes is for a couple of millimetres of snow to settle in Central London and you'd think the Blitz was back on. The rail network grinds to a halt and the scarcely believable news that a country in Northern Europe gets a bit chilly in winter becomes the top story on every news bulletin. Meanwhile, us northerners look on and wonder why we didn't get on the news when we had that nasty cold snap last week.

Ultimately, if we want to make ourselves feel better about our very slightly colder climate, perhaps we should stop comparing ourselves to our southern neighbours. Rather than covering the whole of the UK, maybe our weather forecasts should cover Greenland, Scandinavia and Scotland before finishing with the North of England. That way they would always end on an upbeat note, with something like, 'But moving on to Cumbria, the picture becomes much brighter, with temperatures reaching as high as minus three around lunchtime.'

# THE NORTHERN MONKEY HALL OF SHAME

This section deals with those who've made enemies with the North for one reason or another. Typically, these cowards will use forums such as newspaper columns and think-tank reports to slag off the North rather than, say, blurting it out in a Rotherham pub and getting the kicking they so richly deserve.

## Kelvin MacKenzie

In a recent column in *The Sun*, MacKenzie advocated building a wall to block out the North. MacKenzie is already as unpopular as it's possible to be up North, as it was under his editorship that *The Sun* ran its infamous front page blaming the Hillsborough disaster on Liverpool fans. So he doesn't have much to lose in making these statements. And while the idea of building a wall to keep out all those braying southern ponces isn't entirely without merit, the cost would probably be prohibitive. But I'm sure if we all chip in we could afford to build a wall around MacKenzie himself. And then maybe chuck in a few angry Scousers with baseball bats.

## Brian Sewell

Art critic who's so posh it seems to be causing him physical pain. He once claimed that an exhibition in Gateshead was too important to be held there and should be moved to London where audiences were 'more sophisticated'.

This might have offended the people of Gateshead, but luckily Sewell is so upper class that none of them could understand a word he was saying.

## Boris Johnson

His middle name is 'de Pfeffel', his nan is called 'Granny Butter' and Londoners chose to put him in charge of their city. Which should tell you all you need to know about them.

Johnson made an enemy of the North in 2006 when he signed off a *Spectator* leader accusing Scousers of 'wallowing in tragedy'. He was forced to visit Liverpool to personally apologize, but his buffoonish efforts to make up were a textbook example of digging yourself in deeper.

> 'That great foul city of London there –
> rattling, growling, smoking, stinking - a
> ghastly heap of fermenting brickwork,
> pouring poison out of every pore'.
>
> John Ruskin, art critic (1819–1900)

## Michael Winner

The portly restaurant critic has described the food in northern restaurants as 'terrible beyond belief'. Although there might be a very simple reason why the obnoxious critic's food tastes a little bit more phlegmy than everyone else's.

## The Policy Exchange

In August 2008, the right-wing think tank suggested in their 'Cities Unlimited' report that northerners should abandon their homes and migrate to the South, because so many northern towns have 'lost their *raison d'être*'. So not only did they piss off everyone in the North, but they managed to slip in a pretentious French phrase at the same time.

The Policy Exchange's advice was so ridiculous that they must surely have had an ulterior motive. They were probably just trying to panic everyone into abandoning the North so they could steal everyone's laptops, go on all the rides at Blackpool Pleasure Beach without queuing and shop at Ikea on a bank holiday weekend.

## Josh Hartnett

American actor who deserves an award for the least convincing northern accent in screen history for the 2001 film *Blow Dry*. Like all films set in the North, the plot involves a lovable underdog triumphing in a national contest, in this case hairdressing championships. Aiming at some kind of Yorkshire accent, Hartnett's efforts are so inconsistent that his character seems to be suffering from a personality disorder.

The only northern accent in cinema history that's anywhere near as bad is that of Juliette Binoche as Cathy in the 1992 adaptation of *Wuthering Heights*. Making so little effort to hide her French nationality she might as well have been wearing a string of onions around her neck and waving a white flag, you could at least say in Binoche's defence that she wasn't really trying.

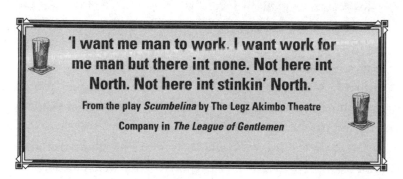

'I want me man to work. I want work for me man but there int none. Not here int North. Not here int stinkin' North.'

From the play *Scumbelina* by The Legz Akimbo Theatre Company in *The League of Gentlemen*

## Matt Johnson

Although the lead singer of eighties rock band The The wasn't openly hostile to northerners, he was notorious for devising a band name that was especially hard to say for anyone who suffers from definite article reduction. Unsure of whether to ask for the latest single by T'The or T'T', northerners plumped for the new Rick Astley record instead, and Johnson's chart positions suffered.

## Hale and Pace

Eighties comedy double-act who in 1987 offended the North with comic song 'Northern Calypso', whose lyrics included 'I come down pub and I have ten pints / Ecky thump, I'm getting plastered / I get back home and I beat up wife / 'Cos I'm a big fat northern bastard.'

It's strange to think that this show was considered risqué and shocking at the time. Watch it today and it still seems shocking, but in a different sense of the word.

## William Hague

Originally from Rotherham, Hague's attempts to make his Yorkshire accent posher left him sounding like a northern ZX Spectrum. When he was elected as Tory leader in 1997, Hague attempted to exploit his northern roots to widen his appeal, claiming that he used to drink fourteen pints in a day, even though it's clear from looking at him that he'd be passed out in the corner of the pub with sick all down his trousers after a couple of halves.

## Margaret Thatcher

Thatcher had a devastating effect on the North in the eighties. She decimated manufacturing industry, crushed trade unions, left communities in a state of neglect and, most unforgivable of all, inspired thousands of terrible plays about how grim life is oop North. No one who ever had to sit through a fusion of experimental theatre and contemporary dance about losing your job and being left on t'scrapheap will ever forgive her.

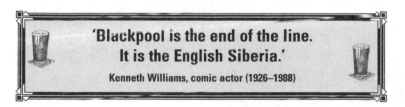

'Blackpool is the end of the line.
It is the English Siberia.'
Kenneth Williams, comic actor (1926–1988)

# A Guide to Northern Accents

Most southerners believe that there's such a thing as a northern accent, and will probably do an impression of one if you ask them, which is likely to be the words 'Ey up chuck' delivered in the style of Geoffrey Boycott or John Prescott. As all true Northern Monkeys know, however, there are many different northern accents, from the high-pitched whine of the Scouser to the flat drone of the Yorkshireman. Indeed, speech patterns have incredible variety in the North, where you can stop your car for directions every half an hour and hear a different accent each time (although all of them will be helpful and friendly, of course).

If you stopped in Liverpool, you'd hear the Scouse accent, which features a range of rising and falling tones that betray an Irish influence. Travel east and you'll start to hear the Manc accent of Liam Gallagher and Shaun Ryder, which is also fast and Irish-influenced, but with slightly flatter vowels.

Travel just a few miles north to Bolton and you'll hear the more traditional Lancastrian accent of Peter and Vernon Kay. Vowels will lengthen, most famously with the long 'oo' sound you can hear in words like book, cook and look, and the word 'were' will replace the word 'was'. You'll also hear t'definite article begin to contract as you head for the Yorkshire border.

Cross it and you'll hear the famous Yorkshire accent with its flat vowels and dropped aitches. Associated with plain speaking, common sense and boasting about how tough you had it when you were a lad, this is the only northern accent most southerners know, because the nearest they've come to visiting the region is watching *Last of the Summer Wine* or *The Chuckle Brothers*.

Head further north, and you'll eventually hear the sing-song tones of the north-eastern accent, where the word 'poem' has only one syllable but 'film' has two. Once derided by snobby southerners, this accent has become the nation's unofficial favourite in recent years. In September 2008, it was named the coolest regional accent in a survey conducted by the CoolBrands Council. A month later, Cheryl Cole and Ant and Dec were found to have the nation's best-loved accent in a poll conducted by Travelodge (although presumably not in

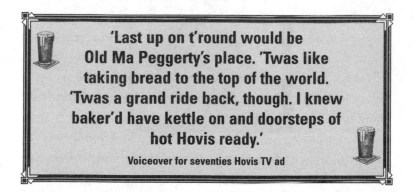

'Last up on t'round would be Old Ma Peggerty's place. 'Twas like taking bread to the top of the world. 'Twas a grand ride back, though. I knew baker'd have kettle on and doorsteps of hot Hovis ready.'

Voiceover for seventies Hovis TV ad

Sunderland). This might explain why the North East is chosen as the location for so many call centres. On the one hand, you've just been dragged out of the bath by someone asking if you're entirely happy with your car insurance. But on the other, they sound like they'd be good for a spot of light-hearted pub banter, so you might as well hear them out.

We shouldn't go too far in supposing that attitudes towards northern accents have changed, though. It's true that you hear more northern voices on the telly these days, but they're still more likely to be doing inconsequential things like narrating events in the *Big Brother* house than grilling the Prime Minister or reporting on a major tragedy.

This view of northern accents as fun but frivolous seems to prevail in the workplace too. In 2005, the Aziz Corporation conducted a survey to find out which accents would most easily lead to business success. It found that while 77 per cent of people considered a south-eastern accent to be a sign of success in business, 64 per cent regard someone with an accent from the North West as unlikely to be successful.

# PUNS THAT ONLY WORK
## IN CERTAIN ACCENTS

While some jokes spread around the country, others don't make it far from their point of conception because they're based on puns that only work in particular accents. Here are a few examples:

### A Joke That Only Works in Yorkshire

A man goes into the vet because his cat is ill. The vet says 'Is it a tom?' and the man replies, 'No, I've got it here in t'basket'.

### A Joke That Only Works in Newcastle

A woman walks into a hairdresser's and says, 'I'd like a perm please'. So the hairdresser starts, 'I wandered lonely as a cloud . . .'

(This joke is sometimes told with a follow-up in which the woman replies, 'No, I mean I want it curled,' and the hairdresser opens the window.)

### A Joke That Only Works in Lancashire

A man goes into a shop and says, 'Short back and sides, flat top, mullet.'

The shopkeeper replies, 'Sorry, mate, I don't speak 'urdo.'

### A Joke That Only Works in the Midlands

Noddy Holder walks into a clothes shop and says, 'I'll have a pair of platform shoes, some flared trousers, a big glittery hat and a shirt with a massive collar please.'

'Kipper tie?' asks the assistant.

'Oh, thanks', says Noddy. 'I'll have milk and two sugars.'

So it seems that the perception of northern accents has changed to a degree, but not when it comes to the important stuff. They might make you sound like you'd be a great company on a night out, but wheel one out in a job interview and you might as well turn up on a pit pony. Whatever you do, though, don't try and force your northern accent into something more posh and southern. You'll only end up sounding like William Hague.

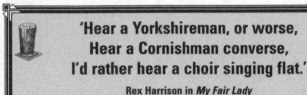

'Hear a Yorkshireman, or worse,
Hear a Cornishman converse,
I'd rather hear a choir singing flat.'

**Rex Harrison in *My Fair Lady***

# NORTHERN GLOSSARY

**Aye** – yes. Popular with both wannabe gangsters and old Yorkshiremen.

**Bairn** – child. A word with Viking origin that lives on in the mouths of Geordies.

**Bangin' or bazzin'** – Mancunian for 'good'.

**Battered** – drunk. Notice how macho northern slang words for intoxication sound, compared to effete southern terms like 'sloshed' and 'trolleyed'.

**Bevvied up** – Scouse for 'drunk'.

**Bevvies** – drinks. As in, 'Yates's are doing two bevvies for the price of one if you get there before six.'

**Big-massive-no-way-fuck-off** – colourful Mancunian expression for describing something large. As in, 'I've just had some big-massive-no-way-fuck-off speakers fitted in my Capri.'

**Bobbins** – rubbish. Archaic word used by northern comedy characters such as Frank Sidebottom and Liam Gallagher.

**Bobby dazzler** – an object that would be precious to someone who watches *Bargain Hunt*, such as a porcelain figurine of an otter or a commemorative Princess Diana plate.

**Borrow** – lend.

**Bonce** – head.

**Brew** – cup of tea. As in, 'Get a brew on, you lazy shite.'

**Brick shithouse** – outdoor toilet and, by comparison, a well-built person. By the way, southerners, this is an old expression.

Don't go taking it as evidence that we still have outdoor toilets.

**Butty** – sandwich. As in 'Ken Dodd's jam butty mines'.

**Buzzin'** – good, high on drugs.

**Canny or champion** – Geordie for 'good'.

**Chip off** – Mancunian for 'leave'.

**Chronic** – used to refer to something rubbish in the North West. The word has also rather confusingly become slang for cannabis due to the influence of US West Coast rap.

**Chuck** – term of endearment used in Lancashire and Yorkshire. Less pleasantly, it can also mean to dump someone.

**Chuddy** – chewing gum.

**Chuffed** – pleased. As in, 'Are you chuffed or something?' and the variation, 'Do you want a chufty badge?'

**Clip** – hit. As in, 'Any more of that bloody cheek and you'll get a clip round the ear, you little bastard.'

**Come 'ead** – Scouse for 'let's go'.

**Cob on** – annoyed. 'Cob', which originally referred to any round object, still seems to be a popular word in the North, where it also refers to circular bread rolls and appears in the expression 'sweating cobs', i.e. beads of perspiration.

**Cock** – confusingly, this can be used as a term of affection in the North, in a similar way to words like 'love' and 'pet'. So you'll have to judge whether someone is calling you a cock in a good or bad way from their tone of voice.

**Crack** – women. An instance of the sexist practice of using any slang for female genitalia to refer to women in general. As in,

'There's always plenty of crack in Wetherspoon's on Fridays.' Can also mean 'to hit someone', as in, 'You do what your mother tells you or you'll feel the crack of my hand.'

**Dinner** – lunch.

**Divvent** – Geordie for 'don't'. As in, Q. 'Who's manager this week?' A. 'I divvent know.'

**Divvy** – Scouse for 'stupid person'. Variations include 'div' and 'the div kids', the class at school who still have to mouth along with the words they're reading.

**Ecky thump** – antiquated Yorkshire expression of surprise. Also revealed by *The Goodies* to be an age-old Lancastrian martial art that involved hitting people with black puddings.

**Ee by gum** – oh my God. Only ever used by southerners to tease northerners.

**Ey up!** – ancient Yorkshire expression. Now only used by ill-informed southerners attempting a northern accent.

**Extra** – over the top. As in, 'What are you being so extra for?'

**Fat knacker** – a fat person. Variations include 'fat waster', 'fat bloater' and 'comedy fat bloke'.

**Fill yer boots** – go ahead.

**Fuck a duck!** – expression of surprise. Came into widespread use through the popular rhyme 'Orgy at the Zoo': 'Fuck, fuck, fuck a duck / Screw a kangaroo / Sixty-nine a porcupine / There's an orgy at the zoo.'

**Gan** – Geordie for 'go'. As in, 'I'm ganning doon the car park to do some handbrake turns.'

**Gear** – once Scouse slang for anything fab and groovy, now more likely to refer to drugs.

**Get** – person. As in, 'You lying get.'

**Gigs** – glasses.

**Gobshite** – someone who talks shit. Like a bloke in the pub who tries to start a conversation by claiming that AIDS was started when a bloke shagged a monkey.

**Grand** – great. Used in Lancashire, Yorkshire and *Wallace and Gromit*.

**Haddaway** – Geordie for 'go away'. Often used to accuse someone of lying, as in the variation 'haddaway and shite'. Not to be confused with the Trinidadian singer who had a hit with 'What is Love?'

**Hanging** – Mancunian for 'unpleasant'. As in, 'Don't buy the chips from the Chinese takeaway – they're 'anging.'

**How** – greeting used by nineteenth-century Native Americans and Geordies.

**Howay** – Geordie for 'come on'. As in, 'Howay the lads,' chanted at St James's Park and in the Bigg Market.

**Intit?** – northern variation of 'innit?' used by northern hoodies, who have a much better excuse to wear to weatherproof clothing all year round than their southern counterparts.

**I've got manoeuvres to make** – an excuse for leaving because you've got better things to do. As in, 'Sorry I can't go to games this afternoon, sir. I've got manoeuvres to make.'

**Jammy** – lucky. As in, 'You jammy bastard. How come you always win on the scratchcards?'

**Kecks** – trousers.

**Kicking off** – starting a fight. As in, 'Barry's going to kick off with some moshers in the park tonight.'

**Lass** – young woman.

**Leathered** – drunk, or beaten up. Or both.

**Leccie** – Scouse for 'electricity'. Yes, southerners, we do have this. And running water.

**Lend** – borrow.

**Lickle** – variation of 'little' used only by Mancunians and three-year-olds.

**Lip** – Rudeness, back talk. As in, 'Any more of that lip and I'll tek me bloody belt to you.'

**Lorra** – Scouse for 'lots of', as used by Cilla Black.

**Mad fer it** – Mancunian for 'I like it'.

**Made up** – Scouse for 'happy'.

**Mam** – Mum. As in, 'Mam, can I have some money to buy some shoes?'

**Mardy** – stroppy. Hence 'having a mard on', which means being in a bad mood.

**Me** – my.

**Mither** – annoy.

**Mortal** – drunk. As in, 'Baz was mortal in Yates's last night. He threw an ashtray at the barman when he wouldn't serve him.'

**Mosher** – name that a scally gives to anyone who likes rock music, whether they spend time crowd-surfing around mosh pits or not.

**Moussie** – Scouse for 'moustache'. They obviously need more than one term for this, in much the same way that Eskimos need several words for snow.

**Nan** – Grandma.

**Narky** – moody.

**Now then** – greeting popularized by Yorkshiremen like Sir Jimmy Savile.

**Nowt** – nothing.

**No need** – that was unnecessary. Often used when someone's just been insulted.

**Oh, aye?** – really? Sometimes used sarcastically, to show you don't believe something.

**Oot** – Geordie for 'out'. As with the ever-popular chant, 'Tits oot for the lads'.

**Our kid** – Mancunian for 'my sibling'. Can cause confusion if you think someone's claiming their brother or sister is their offspring and try to work out how old they must have been at the time of conception.

**'Ow do** – Yorkshire greeting. Became a catchphrase via the Mel B character in *Bo Selecta*.

**Parky** – Yorkshire word meaning 'cold' rather than 'veteran chat show host'.

**Peppered** – Mancunian for 'skint'.

**Pet** – Geordie term of endearment.

**Pig in knickers** – an unattractive girl, a munter. As in, 'Liam copped off with a right pig in knickers in Voltz last night.'

**Pop** – fizzy drinks, especially low budget brands like Barr, R. White's, My Mum's and Panda.

**Pure** – lots of. As in, 'There was pure fit girls in Elementz last night.'

**Rompidedoodah** – Yorkshire slang for 'sex'. This brilliant euphemism is probably the reason they have more sex in Yorkshire than anywhere else in the UK, according to a recent survey.

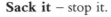

**Sack it** – stop it.

**Scally** – better known as 'chavs' down South. The northern variation sounds slightly more affectionate, as though local gangs who demand money to mind your car are merely lovable scamps.

**Scran** – food.

**Screwing the dole** – Scouse phrase meaning to sign on while taking cash-in-hand work at the same time. Funny that they need a special phrase for this.

**Scrote** – a more insulting word for scally. As in, 'Stop siphoning petrol from that car you lickle scrotes.'

**Set** – the correct northern collective noun for twats and bastards. As in, 'They've suspended me housing benefit. What a complete set of bastards.'

**Shite** – shit. As in 'bag of shite'.

**Skinful** – enough alcohol to make you drunk. As in, 'I'm going down the pub to get a skinful.'

**Snidey** – another Mancunian word for untrustworthy.

**Soft** – can refer to physical weakness or stupidity, as in, 'Kids these days have all gone soft.'

**Sound** – alright. As in the Scouse expression 'sound as a pound'.

**Sorted** – good. As featured in the Madchester-era phrase 'top one, nice one, sorted'.

**Southern Jessie** – the opposite of a Northern Monkey. Also known as a Southern Fairy, Southern Softy, Southern Shandy-Drinker or Southern Ponce.

**Spark off** – start a fight.

**Spark out** – punch someone.

**Spawny** – lucky.

**Starting** – initiating a fight. As in, 'Are you starting or what?'.

**Summat** – something.

**Ta** – thanks.

**Tab** – cigarette. As in, 'Will you buy us some tabs if I give you the money? The newsagent won't serve us.'

**Tarra** – goodbye.

**Tea** – refers to an evening meal as well as a hot drink.

**t'Internet** – the Internet. This particular example of definite article reduction has caught on thanks to a Peter Kay stand-up routine in which his gran asks him, 'Are you not on that t'Internet yet?'

**That London** – London, the capital of England, that place where they're all la-di-da.

**Top** – good.

**Townie** – an older variant of the word 'chav'. The kids who hang around in town spitting on people's heads from overhead walkways.

**Trackie** – Scouse for 'tracksuit'. Again, it's funny how they need a slang term for this.

**Trollies** – underpants. Hence the hilarity when a stag party spot a 'No trollies past this point' sign at an airport and take photos of each other mooning next to it.

**Us** – our. As in, 'The *Grease* megamix is coming on. Let's dance round us handbags.'

**Trapping** – going out on the pull.

**Wag** – used to mean taking a day off school or work, now refers to the wives and girlfriends of footballers or the *Heat*-reading receptionists who aspire to this vacuous lifestyle.

**Weary** – boring.

**Were** – was.

**Whyaye man** – Geordie for 'yes'.

**Wor** – Geordie for 'our'. Hence the joke about General Custer at Little Big Horn in which he says, 'They've got war drums,' and a Geordie soldier replies, 'Thieving bastards.'

**Yard** – garden.

**Yaright?** – Mancunian greeting.

**Yoose** – the correct Northern plural of 'you'.

## 'The North will rise again'

**From the song 'The NWRA' by The Fall**